Sydonnne

I hope you enjoy this book as much as I enjoyed writing it!

[signature]

10.10.14

x

Inspired by Reiki Energy

Jacqui Gayle

ISBN: 978-1-4525-5094-7 (sc)
ISBN: 978-1-4525-5093-0 (e)
ISBN: 978-1-4525-5092-3 (hc)

Library of Congress Control Number: 2012907348

Balboa Press books may be ordered through booksellers or by contacting:

Balboa Press
A Division of Hay House
1663 Liberty Drive
Bloomington, IN 47403
www.balboapress.com
1-(877) 407-4847

Printed in the United States of America

Balboa Press rev. date: 02/10/14

Dedication

To my dearest friend, Karen Louise Beesley, who fell asleep on October 7, 2010. Karen was the person who initially motivated me to write this book.

Contents

Foreword

Jacqui and I have been friends for more than twenty years. We first met when Jacqui was training to be a Samaritan volunteer, and I was asked to be her tutor.

From the very first meeting, we both felt that we knew each other, and jokingly, we said that we must have "met in a former life."

I have seen Jacqui grow into a confident person who believes truly in all she teaches and has a positive approach to life. I have the privilege of being godmother to her beautiful daughter, Simone. Jacqui is a real family person, and her family always comes first—and rightly so.

As I read this book, I realize what a remarkable journey this has been. She explains in layman's terms with depth and feeling the mystery and history of Reiki, which has helped me to understand it more. This is a powerful account of her unflinching faith in herself and God. I'm respectful and proud of what she has achieved. Everyone will come away with something from this book, and I hope it will all be positive to those guided to it.

Thank you, Jacqui, for giving me the privilege of writing this foreword.

Peace and Love,
Marilyn

Acknowledgements

I will not even attempt to list everyone who helped me with this book. I am grateful to all my personal Usui Reiki teachers, students, and clients. My sincere appreciation goes to my family and friends for their love and support. Special thanks go to Jane Wenham-Jones and Oliver Harper for their continuous motivation; Helen Steiner-Rice, Dorothy Lingg at Helen Steiner Rice Foundation; the Verulam Writer's Circle, who gave inspiration and guidance, the Reiki Council; and not forgetting those with outstanding contributions: Debbie Purser, Erica Gadsden, Derek Spriggs, Jan Barrows, Susan McKevitt, Marilyn Gearing, and Balboa Press.

Introduction

My motive for writing this book is the desire to help others gain as much happiness and success from life as I have. I have found that in today's world, we are taught to be skeptical; we are taught to doubt and not to believe without seeing. But for me, it's all about trust, trusting in the power from within.

If you're looking for some inspiration, a good read, or insight on the Reiki system, you have come to the right place. Those who are still asking, "What is Reiki?" have also come to the right place. Reiki is one of the most effective stress-reduction and relaxation techniques available to modern mankind.

We all have the ability to tap into universal energy to some degree, and I have experienced this power of technique to help others and myself. Using Reiki, it is possible to regain balance emotionally, physically, and spiritually from within. One never needs to be ill to receive Reiki treatments, however receiving treatments can help restore and balance any depleted energy within our bodies.

Scientists are only beginning to acknowledge a fundamental link between our minds and the material universe, recognizing that our thoughts affect this great energy field that we all belong to. The Japanese *kanji* on the front cover of my book stands for enlightenment, which literally means "to see things in a new light" or even the attainment of spiritual insight.

I am a woman with the determination to help others in the process of helping themselves. The techniques of the Reiki system can put us in touch with our real selves by expanding our awareness and enabling us to become sensitive to the "life force" running through all living things.

In this book, you will find practical ideas, techniques, exercises, and principles to enable you to enhance your life.

In this book you will also learn about my privilege to study Reiki with five outstanding Reiki masters and teachers: Wendy Bradley, Frans & Bronwen Steine, Mr. Tado Yamaguchi, and Maureen Gardner, who introduced me to Reiki and shared healing with me. Gaining this tremendous wealth of Reiki knowledge has enabled me to write my story. This book promises an easy-reading life story with a twist of Reiki history.

The spiritual path I have taken as a Reiki practitioner has expanded my awareness, allowing me to take a good look at and within myself and to be able to change the things that I did not like and that no longer served me well. In turn, this empowered me to enhance the things I did like.

Reiki is a complete method for activating natural energy to promote healing, enlightenment, and personal growth. I understand that using the principle of meditation to assist in stopping the internal chatter that goes on within the mind is not an easy task. However, with practice and persistence, it is possible to achieve this.

It is my hope that this book will give insight to those who are seeking Reiki energy in healing or learning and will offer a better understanding of how we can bring joy and happiness to our lives. It is an honest book, a description of the guidance and knowledge that I received.

I am proud to be a British writer sharing principles and skills that can be learned by all. Please feel free to contact me if you have any questions or if I may be of help in any way. Visit my website at www.time2heal.co.uk or visit my blog at www.jacquigayle.com.

CHAPTER ONE
Walking the Reiki Path

MY STORY

In the spring of 2008, I was at Heathrow Airport, in London, England, waiting for a plane to take me to Japan. My thoughts ran away with me. *How on earth did I become so blessed?* I was about to embark on a journey halfway around the world. So I went and bought a notepad and began to write.

Back in the early nineties, my marriage was falling apart. I had, by this time, my fourth and last child. My husband, Michael, and I were no longer seeing eye-to-eye. We argued and shouted at each other over the slightest things. We were both working full time: Michael was a driver for the ministry of defense and I worked as a wine consultant for a German company based in London.

My boss at this job kept me away from the other consultants during my first two weeks on the job, and he taught me what I needed to know about wine and how to sell it. I had been a sales distributor for the Amway corporation many years before, but I think my boss saw the potential in me. He taught me the names of grapes and which region they came from. Once the two weeks was up I was allowed into the fold, so to speak. My boss led me into a huge open-plan office where he introduced me to the rest of my colleagues who happened to be all men; being the only female did not bother me in fact I quite enjoyed it. At this time, I worked on Mondays and Tuesdays in the office and spent the rest of the week out on the road, visiting clients.

At this time I was also doing voluntary work as a Samaritan (in some places, the Samaritans organization is known as Befriender International). The Samaritans is an organization that helps people who may be feeling suicidal. Never did I realize how much my Samaritan training would serve me in later years. As a Samaritan, I acquired many skills, including my listening skills.

I'm a great believer that, once we have learned a skill, we need to use it regularly to develop and stay in command of it. The art of listening to others is to focus on the person who is talking. True listening is completely different from simply hearing sounds with your ears. Hearing is a passive and subconscious use of your ears, while listening is an active and conscious use of your mind while listening. With our callers, it was essential to listen actively. The purpose of listening in a Samaritan context was to fully understand the situation of the person who had called in and give them the space to understand themselves. As an active listener, I would use phrases like "hmm," or "go on" to encourage the caller to continue speaking, especially if the caller was nervous or frightened.

Samaritans need certain qualities that callers could recognize and respond to—qualities that help build trust and rapport with the callers. I had to communicate to callers that I respected their views and was interested in them and their situation and that I was listening to them in the present moment, concentrating on what they were saying, and picking up on their comments and concerns. It's a wonderful feeling, being in a position to help others.

Back at home, though, the pressure was intense, and as time went by, I became increasingly unhappy. As a family, we were existing but not living a full and happy life, one of my lifelong goals. Then it became obvious that Michael was no longer committed to our marriage.

A woman sometimes called the house, wanting to speak with him. I confronted her about the situation, and she confirmed that she was interested in a relationship with Michael. I decided I could no longer be treated with such disrespect. I was forced to think of my well-being, and, after discussions, he left me with no other option but to get myself out of the situation by divorcing him.

We had four children to support—Daniel, Andre, Anton and Simone—and a mortgage to pay as well as the usual, everyday living expenses, but I was simply not able to focus on what was going on around me. The deep unhappiness within myself gave me cause for concern. I felt as if I was wandering in a desert, and I needed to find an oasis, a place of calm.

I wondered how on earth we were going to cope.

I did not know where to turn. My mother had passed away, and my father had remarried and moved back to Jamaica.

Although I had what you might call a head start in life—both of my parents were positive people—now that I was all grown up and married, the only person I could talk to who would listen without judgement, and who had listened before, was God.

My mother had been a beautiful woman with the most amazing personality, and I loved my mother very much—but I was always a daddy's girl. My father had introduced me to God, although, back then, I never met him, I was taught to believe he was there. As a baby, I was christened at the local Methodist church, I went to Sunday school at the local church of England, and I was confirmed church of England. As an adult, I was baptized under water in a Pentecostal church.

And so, feeling alone, I went upstairs to the bathroom and began to cry. It was the first time I had cried while praying. I pleaded with God to help me and guide me. God had always answered my prayers before, and I believed that he would answer them now. I told him that I was no longer happy in my marriage, and I wanted the marriage to end. I told him that I trusted him to look after me, and I believed that he would give me the strength to bring the children up on my own if necessary.

This was the first time in a long time that I had prayed and asked for anything specifically for myself. I usually prayed for other people. My father, a deacon in his church, used to tell me that the Lord knows exactly what you want before you ask him.

When I left the bathroom, I thought no more of it and carried on with the rest of my day. A few days later, one of the children caught a really bad cold, so I called the doctor's office and was told I could see a doctor that evening. Michael had done his disappearing act, so I had to take all four children with me. After a little wait, we were called, and I remember being surprised when I walked into the room expecting to see Doctor Raj, my usual doctor. Instead, there was a new doctor, a woman, sitting in his chair. She explained that she was filling in temporarily, and her name was Doctor Tew.

The first thing she commented on was how well-behaved my children were. We then discussed coughs and colds. As she wrote out the prescription for my child, she asked me whether I worked. I thought this was a strange question for her to be asking, but I told her that I was a wine consultant. Doctor Tew asked me to explain to her what this involved, and I told her that I visited corporations and private homes and gave wine tastings to people who enjoyed good quality wines.

Doctor Tew went on to say that she was holding an open day at her home in Woburn and her son Justin, who was a local artist, would be exhibiting his portfolio of work. A few other friends of hers who were involved in various other trades, including books and crafts, would be selling to her invited guests as well. She asked me if I would be interested in coming along to give a wine tasting to her guests. I replied that I would love to come, so she gave me her card and wrote the date on the back and said, "see you there."

I thanked her and left with the children. It was very refreshing to find a doctor who had time to talk to make one feel like a human being rather than a patient.

A few weeks later, the day arrived. I had gotten organized and arranged for Michael to look after the children. I did not know what to expect, but I trusted that everything would be all right and I would sell lots of wine, making a healthy commission.

I set off for Woburn, an area with which I was fairly familiar. My job as a wine consultant covered the whole area of Hertfordshire, Bedfordshire, and Buckinghamshire.

When I arrived at Doctor Tew's house, she asked me to call her Josephine. She introduced me to her son Justin, who later went on to paint me a picture of a rhinoceros, which I still have hanging in my hallway to this day.

I was shown into a little room off the main room, where I could set up my wines. Everybody else was in the main room, and I remember thinking that, even though this side room was beautiful—its bare brick walls set the right ambiance for the wines, almost mimicking a traditional wine cellar—nobody would see me in there.

During the course of the day, I saw people coming and going, but nobody came into my area. A few hours passed, and still nobody came. I was beginning to think that this had been a wasted journey.

I did not know this at the time, but this is when my life changed forever.

Josephine came in with a lady called Maureen, whom she introduced to me. She then left us to talk. About a half-hour later,

I realized that I was doing all the talking, and Maureen was doing all the listening. I had told Maureen how I had lost my mother the previous year, and I had lost my former job working at the Citizens Advice Bureau, and my marriage was failing. In fact, I told her everything. This complete stranger now had my whole life story—in about one hour.

Maureen turned to me and said, "You sound like you could do with some Reiki."

"Reiki! What is Reiki?" I asked.

Maureen told me that it was a form of natural healing, and, because I'd had so much happening in my life recently, I could benefit from it.

At this point, I was willing to try anything. So Maureen gave me her card and said I could call her when I was ready for healing.

There are many types of Reiki available, and, at first glance, this may cause confusion. It is worth bearing in mind that whatever style you receive or be shown how to use, Reiki will always use the same energy—the only difference will be in the method used. It is said that Reiki is intuitive. It goes wherever it is most needed, working on all levels of the body, both physical and emotional. Research has shown that it can speed up the healing of wounds, reduce stress, lower blood pressure, and even help in the management of pain.

When I thought about it, Reiki reminded me of what my father used to do for me when I was younger and had a headache or pains from my period. He would lay his hands on the area of my pain until the pain subsided. I did not realize that some people did this laying on of hands for a living.

The wine tasting session came to an end, and the only person who bought any wine was the doctor. This did not concern me too much, as I could not wait to get home to tell Michael about Maureen and this Reiki thing.

On the way home, I started to convince myself that Reiki might be able to save my marriage. I got home, tired after a long day, and the children were all tucked into bed. I was so excited that, while trying to explain Reiki to Michael, I got tongue-tied and mixed up all my words.

I said to him, "Michael I met the most amazing lady today. Her name is Maureen. She's a reflexologist, podiatrist, and a Reiki master."

"Oh yeah?" he said. "And how much wine did she buy?"

I told him that she had not bought any wine, but that she had said that Reiki healing might help us.

Michael's response was predictably negative. He said, "Us! Us? Don't bother with no us!"

I pleaded with him to give it a try. He wanted to know how much it would cost, and I told him it was thirty-five pounds a session, but that if we booked three at the same time, it would only cost ninety pounds. Michael did not like the idea of spending ninety pounds on something he did not understand.

I told him that I was going to book an appointment for us, as it was worth a try, and I did not know how much longer I could go on living with him like this, what with his bad temper, his drinking, and his smoking.

His response was to do as I "fucking liked." So I added his swearing, especially in front of the children, to the long list of issues I had with him. After that, I had the silent treatment from him, and we did not speak for days.

Michael was not a mixer and did not dare to talk to anybody outside of the family whom he believed to be intelligent. He would say, "I don't know how to talk to people like that."

I was still willing to give it a go, but at the back of my mind, I was afraid that it was not going to work. Michael and I had drifted too far apart. We had stopped listening to one another, and we were no longer creating a life together. We wanted different things. I wanted to be at peace and be happy from within. Michael was in the process of heading into a downward spiral in his life, and the only person that could really help him was himself. Please don't get me wrong here—I'm not trying to make him into a villain, as he was a good father to our children. I simply believe that he had lost his purpose in life. I, on the other hand, felt let down, rejected by the person with whom I'd been sharing my life. My whole body became full of stress, and I could hardly wait for our Reiki appointment.

Isn't it strange that it's only when we are ill that we become aware of our bodies and how we are feeling? Why is it that we never stop to think about healing ourselves—we are, right away, on the phone, making appointments to see doctors or people we consider to be experts. We don't bother to take time to gain knowledge of our own bodies, to see if there are ways other than swallowing antidepressants or painkillers. We walk away from taking responsibility for ourselves, believing that others are more qualified to make us better.

We create stress by overloading our bodies with unnatural chemicals that can be dangerous and lead to a hardening of the arteries or developing into strokes and heart attacks. Good ways to relieve stress include getting plenty of exercise—swimming, jogging, or taking long walks—or taking up yoga, meditation, or just taking time out to completely relax your whole body. We need to consider letting go of some of the control we hold onto and creating fewer demands on ourselves.

I'm not saying that we should not begin with medical check-ups; there are certain conditions that need to be addressed. But once our doctor and medical experts find no identifiable illness, we need to consider alternative ways of healing ourselves. Our bodies need decent fuel in order to operate properly, so it is important to eat a healthy diet. This affects our brains as well as our bodies. It is also good for us to take vitamins or supplements to enhance our well-being. Vitamin C or multivitamins can be taken daily.

I only started taking vitamins when I found out I had a B12 deficiency. I was unable to absorb vitamin B12, which we get from eating meat. It's an essential nutrient, required for the normal activity of our nerve cells. Severe B12 deficiency can cause anaemia, which is not a disease in itself but a feature of many different disorders.

There are various types of anaemia. My type is called iron-deficiency anaemia, and it comes about when the stomach fails to excrete a substance called *intrinsic factor* that our body needs for efficient absorption of vitamin B12. The lack of iron prevents the bone marrow from making sufficient haemoglobin for the red cells in our bodies. I now have B12 injected every three months at my doctor's office.

Here is a quick exercise to help with bringing about and sustaining good health:

Find a place where you can be safe and secure, somewhere you will not be disturbed.

It will make no difference whether you sit or lie down. Close your eyes and breathe deeply from your abdomen rather than your chest. Let the air fill your abdomen, feel your abdomen expand. Relax completely.

Start by summoning a ball of white vortex energy; imagine it spinning at the top of your head. Draw this spinning vortex down, through your crown at the top of your head, and down into every place in your body—right down past your

neck, throat, and into every nerve cell and their far reaching fibers.

Relax your shoulders while continuing to draw this white ball of energy down your upper arms, through to your forearms and hands, and through every system in your body, right down into your thighs, then along your lower legs to your feet.

Now, I want you to think to yourself, "I am breathing healing light into every part of my body. I am perfectly well, and there is no anxiety running through me whatsoever. I am whole and at peace with myself."

Continue to relax every muscle as this white energy vortex travels through your whole body.

Now, stay in that space for five to ten minutes each time you do this exercise. When you're ready, open your eyes and carry on with the rest of your day.

For those of you who cannot see a white light, don't worry—just believe that it is there. The main purpose here is to completely relax your whole body for five to ten minutes per day, convincing yourself that all is well. The more you do this exercise, the better you will feel. If you cannot find any time during the day, try making it the last thing you do before you go to sleep.

We need to focus our minds on being healthy rather than on illness. We need to become health-conscious by holding mental pictures of vibrant health. And we need to promote physical and mental well-being. Learn to think happy thoughts about self and other people; feel good about others and yourself.

If you've heard this once or a thousand times, think positively as much as possible, no matter what the situation may be. I have met many people who have said that they don't believe in all that think positive stuff, and I look at their lives and understand why they are how they are. I'm not saying it is easy to think positive thoughts all the time, but if you're one of those people who keeps saying you don't believe it then it will never work for you. For anything to work, it first needs to be believed. I cannot say it any plainer than that. Do whatever you need to do to make yourself feel good.

The best medicine I have always found—that works instantly—is a dose of smiling. Smiling will always boost the way we feel. Your body becomes more relaxed when you smile. This contributes to a stronger immune system, clears away any tension, changes your emotional state, and allows you to see the universe as a happier place to be.

When my kids were growing up, they were always asking, "Mum, why are you smiling?"

My answer would always be "because I want to." You see, you don't have to have a reason to smile—you can smile just because you want to. I believe that there is an attraction factor with smiling. People will be drawn to you when you smile. Smiling can light up a room and keep you feeling young and very, very happy.

The next step from smiling is laughter; we often laugh because we are happy or someone has made us laugh. Laughing can help make us healthy, as it releases endorphins, small protein molecules that are naturally produced by cells in our nervous system and other parts of our bodies. Endorphins can control pain and reduce feelings of stress and frustration. Just like any aerobic exercise, laughing will increase our heart rate, which, in turn, will make us feel better.

Part of my purpose in life is to contribute to the empowerment of others with my talents—and part of my talent is to make others feel better about themselves. I enjoy making others laugh, and by laughing, we send more oxygen to our brains and the tissues within the body. So, once you get the handle on smiling and laughing, the next natural step is to become and be happy—happiness is a beautiful state of being. Be influenced by happy people, empower yourself with happiness—as one saying goes, always look on the bright side of life.

There are many self-help books that emphasize material wealth and getting what you want materialistically. Yes, the thought of being rich may make you feel happy, but it is just a thought. Unless you can use that thought to create the wealth, it will only be a period of time before you become unhappy again. It is possible to be rich and happy, however, believe it or not, there are also many wealthy people who are very unhappy. There is absolutely no reason on this earth why any of us should be unhappy. There will always be pain and suffering, but that is not a reason for unhappiness, and neither is not having enough education or not having the latest iPad. Your happiness should not depend on what others think or do but on what you want to think and do.

SPIRITUAL KEYS

- *Once a person has been attuned to Reiki, that person is able to give Reiki to others. However, if a Reiki practitioner gives Reiki to the general public, he or she must hold Public Liability Insurance.*
- *The practice of using Reiki as a complementary therapy is increasingly popular in hospitals, general practice offices, hospices, cancer support groups, HIV and AIDS centers, prisons, and private practices all across the world.*
- *Reiki works effectively alongside orthodox healthcare and natural remedies.*
- *Reiki is deeply relaxing and has a profoundly calming effect, which may be experienced as a flow of energy, mild tingling, warmth, coolness, other sensations—or, indeed, one may feel nothing at all.*
- *When you receive Reiki treatments, your emotions may be affected. These emotions may help you experience negative feelings that could have been suppressed in the past, such as fear, sadness, or even anger.*
- *Never forget that Reiki energy is a safe and gentle complementary therapy. It is not an alternative to conventional medicine. If in doubt, always consult your general practitioner.*

Chapter Two

Life-Changing Reiki

Receiving Treatment

Finding a Reiki practitioner can be a little confusing for beginners. Well, let me tell you, they are everywhere, and there are many different styles of Reiki to choose from. The Internet is a good place to start if you do not have a personal recommendation. A good Reiki organization will have a list of professional, insured practitioners. It is important to find someone with whom you feel comfortable, so you might want to meet more than one.

The day arrived for my appointment, and Michael and I went together to Maureen's house. She lived in a small village called Woburn Sands, in Bedfordshire. As we arrived, the tension was palpable. We were ten minutes early, and, as we sat in the car, I felt apprehensive, not really knowing what to expect. We sat in the car in silence, staring out of the windows, and not a word passed between us. I finally broke the silence and suggested that we go and knock on the door. We stood at the front door staring and waiting as if the door might open of its own accord. Each of us was waiting for the other one to ring the doorbell.

I finally rang the bell, and Maureen answered the door with such a warm and welcoming smile that I immediately relaxed. She asked us to come in and inquired which one of us would like to go first. Michael and I just looked at each other and then I said for Michael to go first. This decision surprised me because, at that point in my life, I was not usually the most patient of people.

I sat and waited downstairs. His treatment lasted ninety minutes, and when it was over, he went to sit in the car. In the treatment room, Maureen asked me for my name and a few personal details. She then asked me to remove my jewelry and shoes. At this point, I asked if I could use the bathroom. I took this moment in the bathroom to pray to God and to give thanks to him for answering my first prayer—when I had asked him for help. Meeting Maureen was the answer to that prayer. It is amazing how each of us has our own belief system.

When I returned to the room, Maureen asked me to lie down on the couch. She asked me to relax, and she explained what she would be doing. The word "energy" stuck in my mind. I felt as if Michael had drained all my energy, and I lay on the couch waiting for a miracle to happen.

Lying there with my eyes closed, immediately I felt an enormous spread of warmth across my face and an inviting feeling of slumber as my whole body relaxed. Maureen started by placing her hands over my eyes, moving around to my temples, then to my throat, behind my head, my heart—then came a new word to me: solar plexus. This is situated just below the heart and above the navel. Then came *sacral,* another new word. This is situated below the navel but above the genitals.

Maureen continued to lay her hands on and down the front of my body. This gave me the sensation of being covered in a warm blanket, and I felt a tingling sensation down my arms and legs. The feeling of warmth disappeared and I felt cold. I mentioned this to Maureen, and she placed a real blanket over me.

By treating the entire body, Maureen was helping to heal whatever was causing any imbalances within my body. With her touch, she was able to align my energy centers, known as chakras. I will speak more about this later on. The only way I can explain how this system works is to say that the practitioner channels the

Reiki energy, from the Universal Energy Field, through the body. This is probably the simplest and most effective way of transferring Universal Energy.

The next thing I knew, Maureen was asking me to turn over. I was not enthusiastic, since I had just started to feel warm again, and I was drifting in and out of consciousness and had lost track of time. The hand positions of the practitioner are a way to facilitate the healing energy. The hands are usually left in each position for anywhere from three to five minutes, with a whole session lasting between sixty and ninety minutes. I turned over, and before I knew what was happening Maureen announced that she had finished and was going to get me a glass of water.

I remember thinking, *Water! I don't do water, I do brandy and coke.* From that day onward, however, I started to drink water daily.

When I got up to take the glass of water from Maureen, I could feel tears welling up in my eyes. I could not stop thanking her. Maureen is the consummate professional, and she was very sympathetic. We talked for a while, and she advised me not to drink any alcohol that evening, as it would interfere with my treatment.

It was time to leave, but I felt that I wanted to stay forever in the calm and safety of this place. I asked Maureen when I could come again, and she told me that I should call when I felt the time was right to make another appointment. Almost immediately, I felt like the Reiki treatment had given me a sense of lightness and well-being, and yes, I was inspired.

When I got back into the car with Michael, I was curious to know what he thought about his treatment. He made his feelings clear when he said, "I didn't feel a thing, a total waste of time and money, if you ask me."

"Okay," I replied, "but would you come with me again?"

His reply was, "No way. It's a load of rubbish."

This prevented me from discussing the subject with him any further.

A few days later, I decided I was ready for another treatment and called Maureen to book an appointment. I told her what Michael had said, and she advised me to let him follow his own path. I was baffled, as I did not understand what she meant by "'his own path." I explained to Maureen that I wanted Michael to come so we could share our healing experience, as I believed it would help us to improve our lives together. We would again both want the same things.

What Maureen said next shocked me. I felt paralyzed. She explained that Michael might no longer want the same from life as I did. If he chose not to come back for another treatment, I should accept his choice. The clarity of her words came to me suddenly. I thought to myself, *she is right. I have no right to force him into something he may or may not want to do.*

I realized that I had been trying to bring Michael into the world I was creating for our family. This was something he did not want, but he was obviously unable to tell me that he did not want it. As a result, he was acting strangely toward me. All of the shouting and swearing and behaving like an adolescent was his way of not dealing with it. I was so bogged down in my own troubles that I had not seen what was right in front of me.

I decided that I was going to go it alone. I booked another appointment with Maureen and afterward started to have treatments on a regular basis. The more treatments I received, the more conscious and focused I became. I started to notice the birds singing in the garden, the different shades of green of the trees. I allowed Michael to do as he pleased, and I got on with what I wanted to do—raising my children. It was as if he no longer existed for me. We were no longer working at the marriage.

I was having treatments once a month, and, with each treatment, I received what I would describe as different "gifts." I could see pictures running through my mind, and sometimes I would see vivid, bright, rainbow colors. They would just appear while my eyes were closed. Sometimes I wondered if this was the state that we enter when we die, a state of warmth, beauty, and tranquility.

Then came an awakening. I decided to go and visit my sister Marva. I knocked on the door, and when she answered, without any preamble, I asked her, "Are you pregnant?"

She replied by swearing, and she asked, "Are you a witch or something? I've just come from the doctor's, and I haven't told anyone yet."

To this day, I do not know where the question came from. I relayed the incident to Maureen the next time I saw her, along with other similar incidents that had to happened to me. She told me that she thought I had had a rebirth, and it was possible that I was psychic. She asked me if I would like to enhance this remarkable power.

"No" was my answer. Psychic powers are natural, powerful instincts and intuitions that we all possess. But I was frightened. I did not want to see bad things before they happened; I did not want to bring bad news to those whom I loved. I saw it as dangerous and harmful. I did not know how to be diplomatic, and I feared that I would spontaneously blurt things out. In reality, I was becoming more spiritually aware and able to tune into information that came from no known source. But just the thought of being called a witch helped me curb my psychic powers, I can tell you that!

At the end of my treatment, Maureen lent me a book called *Mind Magic (The Key to the Universe)* by Betty Shine.

This book was fascinating. I read it from cover to cover, and when I returned it to Maureen, I immediately took another copy of it out from the library. I had it renewed twenty-nine times, until the librarian asked me if I would like to buy it as I was not giving anybody else the chance to borrow it. I paid him the money, and the book was mine. I now use a few of the exercises that Betty recommends with my Reiki students. I show them the book and explain that I have taken particular exercises from this book.

The time was right for my marriage to end, and we agreed on an amicable split. As I was now on my own, it was impossible for me to continue with my job as a wine consultant—there would be nobody at home to look after the children in the evenings.

When my divorce decree came through, I was thrown for a loop. Once I had dropped the children off at school and daycare, I sat down, overwhelmed with a sense of sadness and numbness. My heart sank, and I telephoned my friend Marilyn. With tears streaming down my face, I told her that my divorce had been finalized and the marriage was over.

Marilyn was a Samaritan herself, and, while she empathized with me, she stated simply, "It's what you wanted, Jacqui." I agreed with this, but I had not expected it so soon. Marilyn assured me that I would be all right; she said, "You have lots of faith."

When I got off the phone, I was plunged into a very dark place, a pit of depression. I sat in the same spot for hours, until it was time to collect the children. I became lonely. The loneliness had a negative influence on my health. My anxiety caused me to keep others at a distance. The days all rolled together, and, before I knew it, a month had gone by. I was capable only of looking after the children, and I certainly could not care for myself. I saw nobody, and I spoke to no one.

Once a month, I dragged myself along to Reiki treatments I could not afford. I was just about able to pay the mortgage and the everyday living expenses, but I had to juggle them. Some days, all five of us would share a tin of beans on toast as our main meal, as money was so tight. The only time I really thought about Michael was in August, when I had to use that month's mortgage money to buy the kids new school uniform. In September, I would get a letter from the mortgage company, reminding me that I was behind.

I remember once asking Michael how he thought I could manage to do everything financially on my own. His reply was, "You'll manage; you always do."

It seemed to me that what he was actually saying was "you made your bed, now lie in it; you chose to go it alone, so get on with it." He probably felt helpless, as he was no longer working and had no hopes of finding employment.

In any case, that was exactly what I did—I managed.

At this time in my life, I truly believed that the Reiki treatments were working for me. They gave me the strength to walk away from Michael and the strength to keep going while I struggled with the children on my own. I kept telling myself that, although it was a long struggle, it would not be forever. I had faith that eventually, things would change for the better.

I used to look forward to my treatments, as I saw them as a sign of empowerment. Maureen would tell me to relax. For a period of around five months, while having my treatments, I would see a recurring vision of myself in the Caribbean with my father, walking along the beach and talking. It was strange because, although I had travelled to Jamaica many times, I never recognized this particular beach. Where my father and I walked, the sea was always to the left of us and the cliff, road, and lush hills were always to our right. When I painted this picture for Maureen, she told me that it was probably because I missed my father. This was very true—I missed him so much that it felt like a bereavement. I honestly thought I would never see him again, but Maureen tried to reassure me that I would see him again.

I could not see past the financial mess I was in, and I believed that I would never be able to buy anything new again.

This reminds me of how I came to meet one of my best male friends.

The main television was in our living room, and I had a portable in my bedroom. But my boys kept taking it into their room, so this portable TV would go back and forth. One day, I looked in the local paper to see if I could find a secondhand TV for myself. I came across an ad for a coin TV. It was possible to rent a TV with a little slot on the side. We'd have to put a one-pound coin in the slot to watch the television. I thought that this was perfect; it would solve the problem. I would not have to buy a TV, and a pound a week was manageable. Only it wasn't a pound a week—it was a pound every time the last pound ran out. This started to get on my nerves. And a man would turn up every so often to empty the slot. The cycle went on, and guess what? The TV set would always shut off when I was watching something really interesting and I had no money left to put in it. Sometimes, I would go for weeks not watching it. Then, one particular day when the slot did have money in it, the stupid thing just stopped working. I had to call the engineer out. I must be honest—I was not having a good day. I complained about the slot being a stupid idea and told the engineer that it would be better if he gave me back all the money I had put in every time he came to collect. He told me that he could not do that, as the boss would not be very happy, I then told him to tell his boss he could come and take the TV and stick it up his ass. With that, the engineer handed me his business card and introduced himself as the director of the company. He wasn't an engineer after all! Well, since I am black, he could not see me blush, but I did go all chocolatey. How embarrassing! I had been thinking I was talking to an engineer all these months and it turns out that he was the director.

That was Peter, and from that day until now, Peter and I have been friends. Whenever I need any kind of help, he is always there for me. Peter became a great part of the support infrastructure that was to help me rebuild my life. It was lovely having a friend of the opposite sex whose only agenda was to help someone he could see potential in.

Lucky for me, Peter owned an electrical shop. Over the years, I went through washing machines, dryers, refrigerators, toasters—in fact, if I needed anything electrical, Peter saw to it that I had it. People might be thinking we were lovers, but believe, me this friendship was built on respect and love.

SPIRITUAL KEYS

- *When in a relationship, be respectful, pleasant, kind, thoughtful, and complimentary to each other.*
- *Never forget to give each other space. We all need a certain degree of grace and dignity. Try hard not to intrude on someone else's privacy.*
- *Realize that you were both independent people before you came together. Try not to make assumptions about what other people are thinking, be honest with your thoughts, and ask questions to make sure there are no misunderstandings.*
- *Communicate, communicate, and communicate. Know and understand what each partner wants from the relationship. Ensure that you are both creating together, sharing the same goals.*
- *When receiving Reiki treatments, the recipient must accept the help being offered and be completely open to the healing.*

Chapter Three
Mind at Peace

Stopping the Internal Chatter

While I was really at my lowest, I read a book called *Talk and Grow Rich* by Ron Holland. This book had been given to me about five years earlier, when I was an Amway distributor. The Amway Corporation was good at providing motivational tools to its salespeople, and although this particular book was not on our official reading list, someone in my line recommended it to me. At that time, I was earning good money, and I did not take the book seriously; I dipped in and out of chapters as I deemed appropriate.

My approach to the book this time was different. I was searching for something more in my life than material wealth. I was looking for peace of mind and happiness; I wanted to conquer the web of depression that I was embroiled in. This time, I started at chapter one, and I began to learn that we in the Western world are basically materialistic, while people of the Eastern world know how to train their minds to achieve incredible feats.

The author explains a formula that can be used to achieve peace of mind, which he calls "silence, stillness, and solitude." He describes this formula as a great power, telling his readers that "all human success and achievement stems from this one power." He goes on to list many famous people who may have used this formula, including Carnegie, Emerson, Mozart, Einstein, Shakespeare, and Edison.

At that time, the only names that I was familiar with were Shakespeare and Mozart. I have since made it my business to learn as much as I can about all of these people.

Reading that book, I saw the words "The secret lies in meditation, in silence, stillness, and solitude." The method employed to achieve this is to take time out to empty your mind. Internal chatter, be it negative or positive, dominates voluntary thoughts that we create in our conscious mind. These may represent truth or untruth. An example of this is when we say we cannot hear ourselves think. Another example is, when we listen to a particular piece of music and, hours later, that same piece of music is still playing in our mind. Then, when we try to focus on something different, it is almost impossible, as the music continues to dominate in our mind. For most people, getting rid of the internal chatter is only possible while they are sleeping. With meditation, however, it is possible to clear your mind completely, allowing only what you want in—and leaving what you do not want out.

I set myself the goal of achieving freedom from my depression and attaining peace of mind. Each day, after the kids had gone to school, I set about motivating myself to try this formula. Following the book's suggestion, the first thing I did was to find a place of my own where nobody would disturb me. This place was my home.

I had stopped going out and mixing with people, as I felt that my personality had disappeared. I was certain that nobody would be calling on me at home. People pick up on negative energy (by negative energy, I mean a negative mindset and attitude) and are disinclined to be around people who are full of "doom and gloom." People generally want to be around happy, vibrant people, as they feed off the positive energy and enthusiasm. This is how I wanted to be again.

I needed to find a place where I could feel calm and completely relaxed, so on the first attempt, I went upstairs into my bathroom and locked the door. I did this to establish ground rules for myself and to set the precedent for the times when my kids would be around. I then sat on the floor, as instructed, legs crossed, back straight, hands gently clasped in front of me, in a basic Yoga position. The secret of the formula was to empty my mind and try not to think of anything; I was to concentrate on one object, which I chose—a lighted candle. I would breathe gently and try to relax while focusing on the burning candle. The author writes that, if, in the meditation process, you can reduce the number of thoughts flowing through your mind, you might be able to eventually get rid of the internal chatter, allowing your mind to become more creative.

It is not an easy thing to achieve, and, for the first few days, I sat, trying to empty my mind, and became frustrated with myself when nothing appeared to be happening. Although I was in the bathroom at the back of the house, I was still aware of the airplanes flying overhead and the children playing in the school field. I was so desperate for this formula to work for me that I stuffed tissue paper in my ears. This was not totally successful, so I invested in wax earplugs which worked a lot better.

Initially, I expected this process to last for an hour, but I quickly realized that this was far too ambitious, so I reduced the time to a fifteen-minute session each day. This was much more realistic, but I still got distracted, so I made the decision to focus on the lit candle while sitting cross–legged, as the author suggested, and staring blankly at the candle flame for a minute at a time. I would tell myself that for the next minute, I would think of nothing. This seemed to work, and each day, I was able to manage it for a little while longer. Gradually, I was able to concentrate on my flame without the internal chatter for increasing periods of time. If occasionally a thought popped into my head, such as what I was going to cook for dinner, I was able to give that thought to the flame and carry on focusing.

Eventually, at the end of six to eight weeks, I was managing thirty to forty minutes of meditation, without thinking any thoughts at all. I felt present, confident, and safe. Then one day, something very unexpected happened while I sat in silence, stillness, and solitude—something that frightened the living daylights out of me. I could feel myself moving, which I thought was my imagination. I quickly dismissed the thought, continuing to focus. Suddenly, however, out of nowhere, I started to levitate, rising off the ground, very, very slowly. It lasted for about forty seconds, and I was so frightened that I scared myself and fell back down, onto the floor. I remember asking myself what on earth had happened! I started to say, "Oh my God! Oh my God!" I then burst into tears. Up to this day, I have only mentioned this to a few close friends. I was so scared that I stopped meditating for a few days.

Levitation is a very real thing not something out of science fiction or science fiction fantasy. Accomplished by a special form of breathing, demanding concentration it is possible to lift oneself by actually raising the frequency of the body's molecular oscillation so that it is able to induce a form of contra-gravity.

I then realized that I was able to blank all thoughts from running through my mind, even without being in a meditative state. This made me feel better about myself. Little by little, I started to draw myself out of my depression. I was more focused, and I continued to meditate each day without the experience of levitation. I found that I could sit for one or two hours, just clearing my mind of internal chatter, coming out of meditation, and getting on with my everyday life—thinking only the thoughts

I wanted to think. If a negative thought stepped in, I would get rid of it at once and replace it with a positive thought instead.

A further help along this path is relaxation. The practice of relaxation works through the release of muscular tension held in the body; it is especially helpful in relieving stress and anxiety. Using simple relaxation techniques regularly will help you to rebalance and replenish your energy and gain a better sense of well-being. Here are some easy steps you can take for a whole body relaxation exercise:

First, find somewhere quiet to sit or lie down, making sure you won't be disturbed. Allow yourself to be comfortable and warm.

When you're ready, close your eyes, breathe deeply from your abdomen rather than your chest, and relax every muscle in your body, starting at your toes and working up to your head.

Now, focus your attention on trying to stop the internal chatter going on in your mind. If you find this difficult, simply allow your mind to take you on a journey of your imagination. Start with five to ten minutes daily, increasing this time as you become more comfortable with the exercise.

While I'm on the subject of mind, there is something else I'd like to mention. I know some of you will have heard this all before, however some of you may not. The subconscious mind acts as a storehouse of knowledge and our past experience. The information that is stored in the subconscious mind helps us to form our conscious thoughts. This is why we need to think positively—what we put in is what we will be able to take out. The subconscious mind is unable to reason; it simply accepts all the information that we feed it, because it is unable to distinguish between what is reality and what is not. Good thoughts, good mind.

The practice of visualization is a good way to program the subconscious mind with repetition of mental images of what it is you would like to bring into your life, including being happy and living in joy. Now the conscious mind is the mind that you are perhaps more aware of—it is the mind you are using now to read and comprehend this page, and it is the mind that gets cluttered up with all the internal chatter, including making everyday decisions and creating negative thoughts. We can also use our conscious mind to make the decision to change the contents of our subconscious mind.

My goal was to get myself employed.. I had stopped feeling self-pity, and my sense of self–worth was slowly coming back; working could only increase my self-esteem.

I decided that I wanted a job where I could interact with the public and not just sit at a desk doing clerical work. To this end, I applied for—and got—a position as a job broker with the Department of Employment. In this role, I was helping others find employment, but I was also helping myself. I got back my self-respect and moved my life forward, taking time out each evening to meditate.

I would say to my children, "Mummy is going upstairs to meditate for half an hour." I would ask Daniel to keep an eye on the other three children while I locked myself in the bathroom with my wax earplugs. I could sit in complete stillness, silence, and solitude—as I could not hear a thing—and meditate. Once I had completed the meditation and returned downstairs, it would take me about an hour to reassemble the house. The kids used this time to wreak havoc, but I did not care—not one little bit! I was achieving so much from meditation.

I have since gone on to find other ways it can be applied. Kundalini yoga is one discipline that comes to mind. With Kundalini yoga, one is encouraged to undertake breathing techniques, followed by a range of exercises to loosen and relax the body in preparation for sitting quietly in meditation.

My own experience of Kundalini meditation was that, after sitting for about thirty minutes, I noticed a change deep in the recesses of my mind, my aura, and my body's internal elements. I become enveloped in a sense of great calm and stillness. Once I maintain this state for an hour, the conscious and unconscious minds begin to blend with one another taking away the internal chatter. After achieving this state, and if it is maintained until meditation has been taking place for a total of two hours or more, it is possible to hold this change in the subconscious mind throughout the rest of the day.

I now use guided meditation in the Reiki courses that I teach to show my clients how they can use meditation to stop the internal chattering.

Over the years, I have spoken to and seen many people who have read books for guidance on how to meditate. There are many motivational books that show different methods of achieving the ultimate aim of stillness, silence, and solitude—and therefore peace of mind. Despite this, people continue to complain and bemoan how hard their life is and how gloomy their existence is. They claim they want to find peace of mind but are not prepared to put into practice the suggestions and work at achieving that peace of mind. All I can say to this is that the proof of the pudding is in the eating, and practice will lead to your goal.

Although I continued to work full time, I still found myself struggling financially. So I got myself a part–time, early-morning cleaning job. I remember having to be up at four o'clock in the morning to be at work at five. The company I cleaned for was easyJet Airlines. As part of a team, I cleaned the main call center plus side offices, which included the desk of Sir Stelios Haji-loannou, founder of easyJet. I was referred to as the "posh cleaner,"

I believe because I was dressed for my full-time job to save time when I got back home to get the children out to school.

It was kind of weird the way things worked out. At easyJet, we were always short–staffed, and my supervisor asked me if I knew anyone who was interested in a job. I thought of my neighbor and friend, Karen, who was a bit reluctant at first, as she was not a morning person, but I soon motivated her into it. Karen became a bit hit and miss; she turned up when she felt like it, but that was not a problem for the bosses, as we were so short-staffed. As time went on, I received a letter from my main boss via my supervisor explaining that pilfering had gone on and that personal items had been taken from people's desks. My first thoughts were that I hope nobody was stealing from the desks I was cleaning. Karen was not in that day, but I relayed the letter to her when I got home that evening. Karen was as shocked as I was, and we both said that as long as nobody accused us personally of stealing anything, we would just carry on doing our jobs. That night, just before I went off to sleep and while I was lying there, my supervisor's face came to mind. She was smiling at me. I became confused, as I could not make a connection at first, but then I started to smile as I remembered her words, "you're far too posh to be a cleaner." I then fell asleep.

The following day, Karen made it to work, and we were cleaning at opposite ends of the building. I was in a training room, and I happened to see an open wallet full of cash lying on the floor. I picked it up, left it on the side, and went straight to call Karen. "Come here," I said, "I want to show you something."

We got back to the room, and I showed Karen the wallet.

"Whose is it?" said Karen.

I looked and saw a man's face on an ID card. We looked at each other, laughed, and said in unison, "Set-up." I then took the wallet and handed it to my supervisor. I explained that I had found it on the floor in the training room. I found it quite strange that she made no comment, not even a thank you for being honest and handing it in. Something was not quite right. Guess what? Two days later, when I got in, my manager came to me and explained that my supervisor, with the rest of her family, had been fired for stealing. He reeled off the things that had been found in her house that belonged to easyJet. My mind raced back, remembering the wallet issue and thinking that, if had I taken the wallet, I would have been fired and she would have gotten away with whatever was going on for a bit longer. My manager then handed me a big bunch of keys and said he would like me to be supervisor.

At that moment, Sir Stelios walked by, staring at me. I remember thinking, *he must be thinking she's far to posh to be a cleaner*. Who knows?

I got some more friends who were in need of part-time work, including my neighbor Maggie. When I eventually decided to leave the job, I handed the supervisor role over to Maggie. But the moral of that story for me was to trust my intuition when it is trying to tell me something.

Our intuition is always communicating with us via subtle signals (sensations, emotions, thoughts, and imagery). It is only when we are relaxed and feeling calm that we will be aware of these signals, and because intuition is a channel of information, it can easily be blocked by the unwanted thoughts already going on in our minds. What we need to do is learn to listen and trust in it, no matter what form it communicates to us in. We need to trust our intuition; the truth is that most of us have tuned out, and we ignore doubt and mistrust it.

With intuition, we have a sense of knowing what is the right thing to do, and we act spontaneously without needing to know why. We can also know when something is not quite right. It is up to us to trust that feeling, which is guidance from within.

To become more self-aware and acquainted with your intuitive self, a good place to start is to become mindful, giving your full attention and concentration to the present moment, focusing on the now. This experience will allow you to clearly notice more of the things that are around you and will help you to remain happy and contented with a feeling of peace and calm within.

Children are very intuitive; they live life freely, sleeping when tired, eating when hungry. Children live in the present. They trust and believe that they can do anything because they haven't yet learned to believe that they can't. One of my twins believed he was Superman and decided to fly out his upstairs bedroom window—a week before we were due to fly to America for a family holiday.

While still working at the Department of Employment, I happened to come across a job vacancy that read "mystery shopper," which sounded quite interesting. The job was working for a company called Maritz Customer Research Ltd., which claimed to be the largest custom research company in the United States and among the top fifteen research companies in the world. Not only does Maritz conduct more than 260,000 mystery shopping experiences a year, it also provides a diagnostic tool to gather information about customer experience at the moment of truth—the interaction between a customer and members of staff. *Very interesting,* I thought. *I could do that.* So I applied and became what is called a virtual customer. It was part–time, and I could choose whichever jobs I wanted to do, working around my full-time job and the children. I mainly visited food outlets while being paid to attend, eat, drink, and claim my mileage.

After a few years, I was asked by Maritz Research to become what is called a music researcher for the Performing Rights Society. My role is to visit venues that play music, which could be anything from a shoe shop to a social club—it could even be a live concert or nightclub—most of the time, it is a venue where live music is being played. While there, I note the details of the music played so that the royalty, which is a sum of money that is paid to the original writer, composers, or artist of any particular song, gets paid. I love this part-time job, as I get to meet so many interesting people. Whereas with the virtual customer role, I am looked upon and treated just like any other customer, when I am doing the music research, the venue knows exactly who I am. I'm known as their visitor; I'm there only to listen to the music and record. Something I do find very funny is the way members of the public perceive me. People often come up to me while I'm working to ask me if I am from the tax office or the social security office. I just smile and reassure them that I'm only there for the music. I remember a visit to a particular gay nightclub, which I thoroughly enjoyed. When I had finished, I found the manager to let him know I was leaving. His answer was, "Good. I'm glad, as you're stealing my limelight."

I couldn't help but laugh at this amazing encounter. Thank you Maritz Research Limited for keeping me employed on and off for over ten years.

Back in Chapter Two, I described receiving treatments and having recurring visions of being in the Caribbean with my father.

Well, after I was made redundant at the Department of Employment, I went to work as a supervisor in the wines and spirits section of a supermarket. There, I met and spoke with a customer called Bob Monkhouse. Bob Monkhouse was a famous comedian and television presenter. I didn't work at the supermarket for very long, and I won't mention the supermarket's name, as my time there was not good. (I heard my in store managers grumbling about a black person having been given the job when the company could have found a white person to do it, so I walked away from that job. I did not need the stress; I had four children and a house to manage.)

I then joined an agency for temporary work, and I got a six-month contract with a company called Sitel Corporation. My job was working on the phone, making calls to customers who once had Sky satellite television but for some reason had stopped subscribing. My job was to call them and convince them to come back to Sky TV. I was doing such a good job that at one point, there was talk about relocating me to Scotland, where Sky's headquarters were located. I knew that wouldn't work with my family commitments, but, as time went on. I was named top salesgirl, as I had converted so many subscribers on my own.

Around two weeks before my contract was due to finish, I took a few days off to look for another job. On my second day off, one of the bosses called me and asked what I thought I was doing. I'll never forget his words. He said, "Jacqui, you are on course to win the free holiday to anywhere in the world."

I thought, *oh my god*—I'd forgotten all about that. It was announced right at the beginning of the contract that whoever did the most sales would win a holiday anywhere in the world. You guessed it! I was back in a flash the next day, and yes, I did win the holiday—and yes, I did choose to fly to Jamaica to visit my daddy.

This was one time that I turned to Michael for help, to ask if he would look after the children. He agreed. I remember only having fifty pounds to my name when I arrived at Heathrow to fly out, and I spent forty-nine pounds of it getting my dad the largest bottle of Martell brandy I could find.

Well, I thought, I didn't need any money—my father lived in Jamaica. What did I need money for? It was the best holiday I had to date. While I was there, my dad said he would like to show me where he and my stepmum would be retiring to, a place called

Prospect in the parish of St Thomas. We made it a day out, as my dad said there was going to be a beach there. Now, if you haven't already guessed, this place was the exact replica of the place in visions I had while having my Reiki treatments back home—the sea, beach, and lush hills were exactly the same, and as my father and I walked down the beach together, I described the vision to him. It was no surprise to him! He kept saying, "How many times do I have to tell you, Jacqueline, you are a blessed child." I suppose this would have been my first conscious encounter of visualization becoming a reality.

Once I returned from holiday, I found myself a new job, working as a customer service advisor for an NTL call center. It was a telephone and satellite company that has now been taken over by Virgin Media. I had some fun there, especially one April Fools' Day, when a couple of colleagues and I decided to play a joke on our call center boss. We collected money to pay for a "'strip o'gram." The young lady turned up in full police uniform, and I showed her to his office as the rest of the staff gathered to watch through his glass office. The lady told him that she was arresting him, as he had failed to stop at an accident that had happened on his way to work. Well, the look on his face! He didn't know what to think, and although he couldn't see us, as this lady was standing in front of him, around one hundred of us were just rolling over, laughing our heads off. I couldn't keep a straight face if you had paid me, but once she took her clothes off, he did see the funny side, and he gave the young lady a kiss for her efforts. When he came out of his office after the incident, we all rushed to our chairs still laughing. He turned to me and said, "Jacqui Gayle, I'm going to get you back for this." I tried to deny it but he knew I was part of it. The good thing is, he never got me back!

Spiritual Keys

- *Take time out for yourself. By doing this, you are showing that you care about yourself. This is self-appreciation, and it is not selfish.*
- *If you are thinking of taking up meditation or you already meditate, keep at it, and do not give up.*
- *The remaining twenty-three and a half hours a day are given over to others, be it our partners, children, pets, parents, or jobs. There will always be demands on us that prevent us from self-appreciation. Persistence is the key; take thirty minutes a day for yourself.*
- *By clearing your mind of all the unimportant internal chatter, you free up space to think clear thoughts about what is important and what you want out of life, be it good health, prosperity, or just good old-fashioned peace of mind.*

Chapter Four

Learning Western Reiki

My Journey

Over the years, I have heard the saying, "'When the student is ready to learn, the teacher will appear." This is exactly what happened in my case, with a lady called Wendy Bradley. At the time, Wendy was going through a very difficult situation that no mother should have to experience. Her daughter Cheryl was dying.

Cheryl had given birth to twin girls, Chelsea and Jodie, in January 1993. Cheryl then passed away suddenly and unexpectedly from a condition called Multiple Endocrine Neoplasia in May 1996.

The night before Cheryl's funeral, she came to me in dream form. I can remember it as clearly today as the night I saw her. Cheryl appeared, looking pure and beautiful. She spoke to me, saying, "I'm all right. Tell Mum not to worry. I'm all right." Then she disappeared. I awoke the next morning not knowing what to say or do.

I had known Cheryl for a while, and we had our twins in common. I was not a stranger to her, but I hardly knew Wendy at all. I wouldn't dare to tell Wendy what I'd dreamed, especially on the day of the funeral. I couldn't bring myself to even mention this to Wendy. What would I say? "Oh, by the way, I had a dream last night, and Cheryl said to tell you …" I just couldn't. My thoughts were that she wouldn't believe me, and I would look stupid, so I remained silent.

Finally, a few weeks passed, and I plucked up the courage to go and knock on Wendy's door. She invited me in, and we talked for a while about Reiki and courses and, although Wendy was the least expensive teacher I had come across, I still could not afford my first Reiki course. My bank account was playing "pay a check, bounce a check." Some of you will understand that situation. I explained my current financial situation to Wendy, and between us, we came up with the idea of paying her what I could afford until I had reached the full payment, and that's what I did.

This was going to be my First Degree Reiki level-one course. It was planned over two days on the weekend. For me, this was like synchronicity—meeting the right teacher at the right time. It is important to talk with your Reiki master before you decide to embark on a class. You need to be able to trust your master, as you will be opening up parts of yourself to him or her. If you have any fears or concerns, you need to be sure to mention this from the outset. What happens in a First Degree class will vary from teacher to teacher. My course was going to be on a one-to-one basis, but some courses are taught in a group, and the day will usually start with everyone introducing themselves, followed by telling the group what led them to Reiki. I was so excited that I was going to learn how to treat myself with this beautiful energy experience. To self-heal is to take responsibility for one's life. We can all benefit from self-healing. Wendy taught Reiki from her home, which at the time was ideal for me, as I didn't have the added expense of travelling.

Life was getting better, but at this stage in my life, I was still experiencing financial hardship. I turned up on time the day we had arranged. Wendy first explained what was going to take place over the two days. Initially, she explained the history of Reiki to me. With the help of what Wendy had taught me and through my own research, I have learned that Reiki is a healing technique that is very simple yet very powerful. "Reiki" is also the word used to describe the energy that Reiki practitioners work with, an Oriental word that represents universal life energy, which is the energy in and around us all.

We have so many different terms for labeling universal life force energy: God , spirit, higher self, and higher source—the list is endless. It is a subject of great controversy, but from a personal point of view, it makes no difference what it's called because it's one of the things in life that belongs to us all. For us to be able to identify our universe, we need to understand and accept that everything and everyone is connected. Our human perception—seeing ourselves as separate—is only an illusion. According to legend, Reiki was re-discovered and developed by Mikao Usui Sensei. I say re-discovered because this universal energy was already ancient knowledge. Sensei means teacher in Japanese. He was also called Dr. Usui, although he was never a medical doctor. Usui was born on August 15,th 1865, in a village called Taniai, now known as Miyamacho. Born into a class system, he received privileged education. Dr. Usui traveled extensively and became well-educated by studying many diverse subjects, including medicine, psychology, history, and religion (Christianity and Buddhism). He also taught many techniques, including meditation and spiritual development. Through research, it is known that he became the head of the Department for Health and Welfare, and in 1914, he became a Buddhist monk. He wrote, "Our Reiki is something absolutely original. Through it, the human body will first be made healthy and then peace of mind and joy of life will be increased. Today we need improvements in our lives so that we can free our human beings from illness and emotional suffering."

Usui's travel and education broadened his life experiences and his understanding of the world and human nature. This allowed him to view the world from various perspectives, leading him to ask the question, "What is the true purpose of life?". He came to the conclusion that the ultimate purpose of life was to attain a state of complete peace of mind.

This led Usui to study Zen Buddhism in an attempt to obtain this peace of mind. He studied aesthetics for about three years without achieving enlightenment. He eventually asked his Zen master how he could achieve the peace of mind he so greatly desired. His Zen master replied that maybe he needed to experience death. This answer surprised Usui, but it allowed him to consider whether this was indeed what needed to happen.

I will talk more about Usui as my story unfolds. The unique thing about Reiki is that it can be learned by anyone, including you. You may use it for yourself, to relax your mind and body, help you to relieve stress, and maintain a healthy lifestyle.

In March 1922, Usui retreated to a place called Mount Kurama, a mountain just outside Kyoto. At this place, he began to fast, in preparation for his death. He undertook a practice called Kushu Shinren, which is a form of meditation. Usui is said to have stayed on the mountain for three weeks. The story is also told that one night, he felt a powerful shock in the center of his brain, and he became unconscious.

Several hours passed by, and dawn was breaking when he finally regained consciousness. When he came around, he was surprised to feel refreshed. Usui believed that during the incident, universal life force energy had penetrated his body and soul, and that cosmic energy and his own energy resonated and he began to realize that the universe was him and he was the universe and he had finally achieved enlightenment. He had finally obtained peace of mind, a state of being that most of us are still looking for.

Wendy went on to explain the meaning of the lineage of Reiki and how it has been passed on from person to person.

Here follows my Western Reiki lineage:

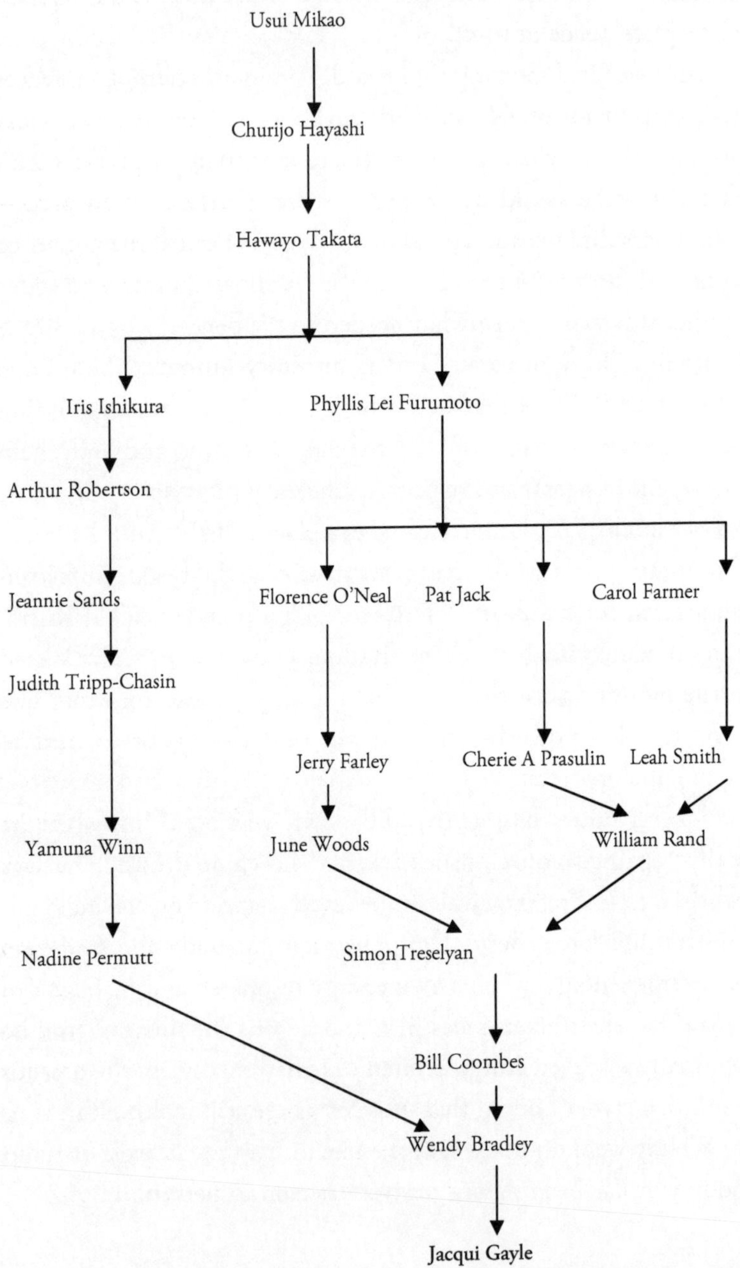

We discussed the word "Reiki." *Rei* is wisdom that comes from our higher self and *Ki* is life force. When something is alive, it has life force circulating through it and around it. When we die, the life force departs. Some people see life force as spirit, and others say that when someone passes away, the "spirit" has left the body. It is this saying that had always led me to believe in a spirit world. I felt that, if the spirits leave the body, they must go somewhere—hence the spirit world. To be honest, I do not know enough of spirit worlds, and I would prefer to leave the dead alone.

From this point, we moved on to the Reiki Ideals, which should be spoken or chanted daily, morning and evenings:

"Just for today, let go of worry, let go of anger. Just for today count your blessings and be grateful to those who have helped you in your life. Just for today go about your business honestly, Just for today be kind to all living things."

I have, from that day forward, taken these words to heart and lived them. I no longer worry, especially about things I cannot do anything about. If I can solve a problem, I solve it. If I cannot fix a problem, I just leave it alone. Worry drains our energy, and it needs to be put into perspective. Anger is a negative emotion, and the only person we harm with it is ourselves; it can affect our well-being and make us unwell. Why not let go of anger today? Try letting go one day at a time. Anger sometimes makes us say and do things we don't mean and that we may later regret.

I now focus on what I do have. I do not pay any attention to the lack of what I don't have. When you focus on the lack of something, you create more need. Give thanks for the people who have helped you in your life, from the postman who delivers your mail to your parents who gave you life and love. Be honest in your daily interactions with other people. If you are honest in your dealings and you expect honesty, that is what you shall have.

Finally, be kind to all living things. Forget the fly spray; open a window. If you buy a dog and decide you don't want to keep it, don't just abandon it in the street; take it to a shelter. Be kind to other people, too—even if they are not kind to you.

This is followed by the first of three or four Reiki attunements, which are spread out over the two days. Everyone will have their own reaction to attunements, and each course will differ, depending on the teacher and the learning tradition the teacher has come from.

Wendy explained what happens during an attunement. This is when a master initiates a student to Reiki. An attunement expands our vibratory rate and amplifies the amount of energy that the body can channel.

At this point, I would like to remind everyone that Reiki is already within us all. A Reiki master is not giving a student Reiki; the master simply helps the students to open themselves to the knowledge that they, too, can heal. The students need to accept that we can be a channel through which energy can manifest, remembering that it is the recipient that is drawing the energy through his or her body.

It is important to be relaxed as possible. To achieve this, it is important to keep your eyes closed during this very sacred ceremony. You will be honoring yourself and your Reiki master while this beautiful process takes place. During the initiation ceremony, your Reiki master will use ancient symbols and mantras. These will act like keys that will unlock and activate for you the Reiki energy. (All will be explained about symbols and mantras later in the book.) The attunement process involves intense focus of the initiating master on the transmission of energy from the universal energy field. With this conscious intent, the master draws symbols behind and toward the student with the repetition of mantras, also blowing energy to the student.

Once I'd received my attunements, I could quite clearly feel the energy in the palm of my hands. This also automatically happens the moment you think about giving or sending Reiki healing. Once attunements have been received, it is traditional for students to self-treat with Reiki for twenty-one days straight, as this symbolically represents the time Dr. Usui spent fasting and meditating on Mount Kurama. During this time, students can experience all types of emotional unrest, including physical ailments that may surface as the vibratory rate of the body changes.

I have since learned that there are some practitioners who claim to teach Reiki via their website. Giving a set of instructions so that students can practice techniques to enable them to channel Reiki is not the way to go, especially when it comes to giving attunements. This needs to be done by a qualified Reiki master. An attunement process should be done in person. The Reiki master has an obligation to the students to be with them and to guide them through this sacred ceremony, to its completion.

Next came the twenty-one day cleansing process. An attunement has a powerful effect on your entire body. During this time, a person may experience joy, tearfulness, runny nose, frequent visits to the toilet, and more restful sleep. Energy will flow freely through your hands whenever you touch with the intention to heal. It is a gracious gift for the rest of your life, and the more you use this gift, the more the energy flow increases. It will never disappear.

Next, we learned the "Chakras." This was the first time I understood what chakras are. Chakras are not used in Eastern Reiki, but they have been incorporated into Western Reiki. There are many chakras of the body, and I will explain here the seven main chakras, as Wendy explained them to me.

- The Root Chakra, which is associated with the color red, is located at the genitals.

- The Sacral Chakra, which is associated with the color orange, is located just below the navel.
- The Solar Plexus Chakra, which is associated with the color yellow, is located between the lower rows of the ribs, just under the breasts.
- The Heart Chakra, which is associated with the color green, is located in the middle of the chest.
- The Throat Chakra, which is associated with the color blue, is located in the center of the neck.
- The Third Eye Chakra, which is associated with the color indigo, is located in the middle of the forehead, above and between the eyebrows.
- The Crown Chakra, which is associated with the color white or violet, is located at the top of the head.

A chakra is an energy center within us all. Chakra is a Sanskrit word meaning wheel. Chakras are also called lotuses. By working with the chakras, it is possible to regulate the flow of life-force energy within our bodies, balancing and creating harmony. When I give my clients a Western Reiki treatment, I follow the chakras in order, starting at the Crown and working down the body to the Root, not forgetting to heal the legs and feet.

Wendy then showed me how to self-treat and how to place my hands on my own body. It is possible to do a self-treatment almost anywhere, even in the bath or shower. When you have some quiet time in the middle of the day or on your lunch break, when you get home from work after a hard day and you need an energy boost, or when you go to bed at night—self-treatment will help you drift off to sleep if you are ill or in pain. When you don't have time for a full treatment, just place your hands where you feel most drawn to; your own energy system will draw Reiki to where it is needed. It is better to have some Reiki when you need it than wait until the conditions are right. You cannot overdose on Reiki, and guess what? The energy will never run out.

I learned that Reiki was for healing not only myself but also the lives of others. By the end of the second day, I had experienced the energy of Reiki, including how to treat others and much, much more.

I would like to share my chakra center healing exercise with you. This exercise will help you activate, strengthen, and develop your seven main chakra centers. Read through a couple of times to absorb the idea.

Lie or sit somewhere you can relax, feeling safe and secure, someplace where you will not be disturbed. Close your eyes and breathe slowly and deeply, letting go of any tension.

Begin by grounding yourself. To be Grounded means to be connected to the earth, to be "'rooted, to be centered within ourselves, and to be in the present moment."

Continue to breathe deeply.

Be aware of your feet, now imagine that your feet are sinking through the floor, into the earth below. See your feet being planted in the earth. Imagine that you are a tree, growing roots down into the earth from your feet. Allow the roots to sink deep into the earth.

Now become aware of the area around your spine, your base chakra. See a red vortex of energy glowing and a feeling of connecting yourself to security and trust. Next, imagine that you are drawing positive energy into this part of your body.

Now become aware of the area just below your navel, your sacral chakra. See an orange vortex of energy glowing and a feeling of creativity connecting yourself to sensuality and

loving relationships. Imagine that you are drawing positive energy into this part of your body.

Now become aware of the area just below your chest, your solar plexus. See a yellow vortex of energy glowing and a feeling of energy connecting you to will power and self-control. Imagine that you are drawing positive energy into this part of your body.

Now become aware of your heart chakra, in the middle of your chest. See a green vortex of energy glowing and a feeling of unconditional love connecting you to love and compassion. Imagine that you are drawing positive energy into this part of your body.

Now become aware of your throat chakra, and see a blue vortex of energy glowing and a feeling of great self-expression connecting you to communication and truth. Imagine that you are drawing positive energy into this part of your body.

Now become aware of the area called the third eye, in the middle of your forehead. See an indigo (which is the color between blue and violet) vortex of energy glowing and a feeling of clear vision connecting you to intuition and your natural psychic abilities. Imagine that you are drawing positive energy into this part of your body.

Now become aware of the area above your head, your crown chakra. See a violet vortex of energy glowing and a feeling of wisdom connecting you to knowledge and your higher self. Imagine that you are drawing positive energy into this part of your body.

Now from your base chakra to your crown, imagine merging all the colors together, giving yourself a feeling of well-being and balance. Stay in this space, just for a while, to maintain this healing process, and imagine that all your chakras are now closing, from the base to the top of your

crown. Once again, you will need to be grounded. Do anything physical—wiggle your toes or clap your hands—then open your eyes and return to clear-cut awareness.

First Degree Reiki teaches one the principles of holistic health and provides guidelines to positive wellness. By using Reiki each day, we can regain and sustain our energy balance, keeping us in touch with the flow of *ki* in our bodies.

My decision to take Second Degree Reiki reflects my commitment to become more involved with Reiki. It was an automatic step for me. The period of time between taking the first degree and second will depend on each individual teacher. For some teachers, it will be three weeks; for others, it will be three months. Leaving time between each degree will help students to adjust to the new energy in their bodies and allow time for them to become familiar with the energy of Reiki by reflecting and appreciating the changes.

This was also the time I learned about the Reiki symbols. There are many. As students, we are taught that the symbols are sacred and must be kept secret. The more levels of Reiki one does, the more symbols there are. The symbols are given to aid the process of healing . The symbols are all written in a Japanese style of writing called k*anji*. One symbol in *kanji* is on the front cover of this book.

Wendy showed me how to draw the symbols in the air with my fingers. Once I had learned the symbols, Wendy talked about how to send distant healing. I wasn't quite sure of what to make of the words "distant healing," which sounded to me exactly the same as "absent healing." My thoughts were, *how the hell can you give healing to someone who isn't present*? Distant healing means sending healing to others or situations—whether in the present, past, or future. It is similar to the way radio signals are transmitted, and it is usually taught at second-degree level.

Distant healing utilizes symbols as a pathway on which the Reiki energy can travel from one place to another. You use the third eye, heart, and throat chakras to visualize the person or situation you want to send healing to. This is also a highly effective technique for dealing with emotional and mental problems. The third eye is to see clearly, the throat is used to name the person, and the heart carries compassion. Some Reiki masters teach distant healing with a photograph of the person whom you would like to send the healing to. The distant healing symbol simply acts as a bridge between our intention and whoever is receiving the healing.

Once I got the hang of it, Wendy gave me the technique to send healing to anywhere in time and space, and I frequently sent absent healing to my father in Jamaica. One has to try to understand that it is all about the intention, although I have heard that there is a fine line between healing and sorcery. My main and only intention was to improve my father's well-being.

SPIRITUAL KEYS

- *If you are thinking of learning Reiki or you already practice Reiki, try to treat yourself with Reiki on a regular basis. Every so often, I speak with students who have been taught by myself or others, and when I ask them if they use Reiki regularly, the answer is usually no. I simply ask them, "How can you heal others when you are not taking the time to heal yourself?"*
- *Every now and then, visit another Reiki master, as a treat to yourself; it will give you a real energy boost.*
- *After giving or receiving a Reiki treatment, offer a glass of water to the receiver, while not forgetting to drink some yourself.*
- *It is a good idea not to drink alcohol after a treatment, as this may interfere with the flow of Reiki energy.*
- *As a practitioner, respect the rights of others. Be aware at all times that you do not manipulate others.*

Chapter Five

Time 2 Heal

My Purpose

In 1999, I was ready to take the Third Degree of Reiki. This is called the master level, and it is designed for those who desire to continue further with their Reiki studies. With this course, I received master and healing attunements and was taught new symbols, experiencing more knowledge and guidance.

I was amazed to learn more about different levels of consciousness. It is said that the human consciousness manifests itself on many levels, usually referred to as "bodies." Each of these bodies has certain functions that can help us achieve cosmic oneness. They can show us fears and tensions that have to be counterbalanced on our way to integration. The first body, our "physical body," is the coarsest manifestation of the consciousness. Its function is to teach us to be totally in the present moment.

The second body is the "etheric body." It has the same shape as our physical body but has no solidity or gravitational pull. The function of the etheric body is to teach us unconditional love—no conditions and no limits.

The third body is called the "mental body." It is made up of thoughts and identified with our minds and our thinking process. The best way to relax our mental body is by meditating, a non-selective awareness—that is, observing our thoughts without identifying with them, and just letting go.

The fourth body is called our "spiritual body." Its function is self-knowledge. This is when we look inside ourselves and search for our inner beings through silent meditation. This is also the body that connects all of the other bodies to the universal energy field. The last body is usually called the "cosmic body," because, through silent meditation, one can merge with the cosmos by letting go of individuality.

By June 2000, I had become a Reiki master and teacher, and although I was giving treatments to clients, I was also ready to teach this wonderful art of Reiki. Wendy taught my Reiki Master/ Teacher course, as she had taught all of my courses. In this particular course, there were four students. Wendy took us to a place called the Tree Cathedral in the village of Whipsnade in Bedfordshire for our master / teacher attunements. This is where I now take my students when they reach master level, for their attunements. It is in a stunningly beautiful setting, and it is a place where one can feel the energy of the trees. Tree energy is very powerful.

After this course, I began to ponder what I wanted to learn next, and I was led to an open evening sponsored by Luton University and a master's degree course run by the KCC Foundation, on systemic therapy, a form of psychotherapy.

Psychotherapy can be conducted on a one-to-one basis, involve couples, or even involve the whole family. Seeking help with life should not be considered an indication of failure, but rather it should be regarded as an indication that you are open to and want to improve your emotional well-being, which is a responsible, grown-up thing to do.

I started my foundation course in September, studying one evening a week. One year later, having passed my foundation course, I was still unsure where this was taking me. I enrolled for a two-year course that started in September 2001. At this time, I was back working for NTL, in the faults department, helping customers with their queries. It was not easy juggling work, clients, university, and four kids, but I did it, and I'm so proud of myself.

During this time, the thought came to me that I could not continue at this pace. Something had to go. Without much further thought, I decided that it would have to be my job. I decided that setting up my own Reiki business and looking after my clients would be my main priorities. So I resigned my position at work, without any idea where the money for the next mortgage payment was going to come from.

On October 1, 2001, I officially started my company, which I called Time 2 Heal. The name had come to me following the 9/11 terrorist attacks. I kept thinking, *It's time for the world to heal.*

If only I could do my little bit to help.

I achieved this aim by starting my Reiki business. I was now in a position to help others. This was also the time in my life when I met a friend and my future husband, Philip. He came into my life just at the right time—I was happy, so my kids were happy.

In the early days, before I had given up my job, clients would come to my home after I had finished the early shift at NTL. I had my treatment couch set up in the dining room, and when the kids came home from school, I would give them "the look" to be quiet while I was giving clients their treatments.

My clients were blissfully unaware of this, lying on the couch with their eyes closed. My children would just creep past, quietly making their way upstairs to their bedrooms, until the session was completed.

Eventually I converted a brick outbuilding at my home into a treatment room with its own cloakroom and toilet. It had been used to house my father's chickens many years before. The outbuilding was cleaned and decorated. Having this separate treatment room meant that my clients no longer needed to enter my home. They accessed the treatment room by coming down the side alley leading into the rear garden.

Once I was officially in business, it was time to let people know. I called the local newspapers and placed advertisements with them. Over the years, other practitioners have said to me that they do not advertise. I am not sure why this is, but advertising certainly worked for me—and continues to do so.

Clients began to come to me in droves. I believe they came because I visualized them coming. I could see them in my mind's eye. I also visualized myself carrying out my daily work; I visualized my plans for achieving a successful practice. My images became more vivid, and I found that my subconscious would throw up more and more images that appealed and aided me in this process. At one stage, I decided I was going to build my own website, so I invested in Microsoft Front Page. I then realized I was only kidding myself, so I enrolled in a free website course that was being run by business link at my local chamber of commerce building.

That was where I met my good friend Karen Beasley, who has now passed away. Karen was the tutor on the course. We "gelled" as soon as we met, and, although I heard every word Karen had said during the course, I just could not get my head around creating a website on my own. Quite honestly, I think it was the fact that Karen was more interested in my Reiki practice and coaching than I was in finding out how to double-click on the index.htm file.

Well, you can guess what happened next. I was giving Karen Reiki and coaching sessions in exchange for her website expertise. Karen was so clever that I would just have to call her up and ask her to make some changes for me, and by the time we had finished talking, she had done whatever I had asked. No money was ever exchanged, and we enjoyed each other's company and became the best of friends.

Another advertising medium that I used was the local radio station. People were not only seeing my advertisements, they were now hearing them too. Seeing and hearing are powerful tools in the process of manifestation, a subject I will talk more about further on in this book.

People came to me for all sorts of reasons but mainly because so many of them felt that they had been let down by conventional medicine, which is supposed to provide scientific answers. Some came because they just wanted to talk to someone, and others came just out of curiosity. As I was charging for my time, the simply curious people did not bother me at all.

To practice Reiki on members of the public, a practitioner must have public liability insurance. As far as I am aware, insurance companies will only insure therapists who are registered with a professional body such as the UK Reiki Federation or the Complementary Medical Association. I held membership with both of these organizations prior to setting up my business.

The UK Reiki Federation was established in 1999 and is an independent association under a national umbrella organization for education, training, and guidance in the public practice of Reiki. Practitioner members choose to adhere to a strict code of ethics. Being a member of the UK Reiki Federation and attending its annual event is an essential and vital opportunity to expand one's knowledge of Reiki.

A very significant and important individual whom I must mention in relation to the UK Reiki Federation is Doreen Sawyer. She is the secretary of the federation, and it is her hard work and dedication to keeping the cogs of this expanding organization well-oiled and in good running order that have contributed in no small way to the success of the federation. Doreen took over the position of secretary in 2002, and it is interesting to note that in 2001, there were 747 members. The membership has increased year after year, to the current membership of over 1,700. This is proof positive of her hard work in promoting a growing awareness of the benefits of the federation to members and other interested parties.

The Complementary Medical Association (CMA) covers a wide variety of therapies under the umbrella of complementary medicine, including aromatherapy, reflexology, and acupuncture. It was established in 1995 and is run by Jayney Goddard, who is the president. Jill Lucas, the chief administrator and Roberta Macmillan, membership coordinator, assist Jayney in the day-to-day operation of the organization. If you call the association, you will probably speak to Roberta, who is polite, friendly, and extremely helpful.

As my business continued to grow, I decided to diversify into teaching Reiki. I must mention at this point that it is important to understand that you cannot learn Reiki from words alone. It is through life experience that you gain the knowledge and expertise to practice.

Some of my students would phone me up and say, "If I come and do my Reiki level one or level two with you, can I start teaching it straight away?"

I would have to explain that they would need time to practice Reiki not only on others but on themselves also, on a regular basis, before they could even consider becoming Reiki teachers. I also firmly believe that before one can call oneself a Reiki master, it is necessary to self-treat with Reiki at least once a day, thereby building up one's own bank of positive energy. Only when we fully understand what Reiki is and how it works to the benefit of self and others do we have the right to call ourselves masters. Many people wonder how a person can learn to practice Reiki healing in two or three days, then go straight into charging the general public money in return for healing treatments. I firmly believe that you should not do this. At present, there is no formal accreditation for practitioners, and this means that anybody can set up a Reiki practice. The General Regulatory Council for Complementary Therapists and other organizations are working to develop national occupational standards in order to improve this situation and help the move toward self-regulation. This can only be a positive move for Reiki, and it would go a long way toward allaying any fears or doubts that members of the public have about the credentials of practitioners.

In line with other professionals, it is absolutely vital that Reiki practitioners should be working toward their own continuing professional development, and this is currently a requirement for membership of the Complementary Medical Association and the UK Reiki Federation.

As part of the code of ethics and practice, I have listed below some key values for implementation for those of you considering practicing Reiki. I have reproduced this courtesy of the Reiki Council.

One must do the following:

- Give Reiki to his or her clients with respect for their dignity, individual needs, and values, and without discrimination.
- Be without judgment concerning race, color, creed, gender, or sexual orientation.
- Provide comprehensive and easy-to-understand information to allow clients to make informed choices.
- Respect the right of the client to choose his or her own forms and path of healing.
- Act honestly and maintain professional integrity.
- Practice only within the boundaries of the Reiki practitioner's competence and qualifications.
- Acknowledge and respect all practitioners and disciplines.

- Work to foster and maintain the trust of clients and the general public.
- Keep all client information confidential unless required by law to do otherwise.
- Comply with the Continuing Professional Development requirements of the "proposed regulatory body."
- Respond promptly and constructively to concerns, criticisms, and complaints.
- Comply with relevant legislation.

I very much enjoy delivering Reiki courses, whether to individuals on a one-to-one basis or to a group. However, my groups only contain up to six students. This is so that I can give individual attention to each student, especially if they have any queries or concerns.

My students come from very diverse backgrounds—from social workers, midwives, directors, and administration staff to people who are just looking for a new direction in their lives. I derive immense personal satisfaction from helping people move forward in their lives, and that is why, in 2004, I decided to become a life coach.

After studying three years at university, I decided not to go any farther with my training as a psychotherapist. I preferred to help with the uplifting of others in a positive and energetic way. Don't get me wrong, psychotherapy is a good thing for those who need it, and I have carried with me the skills I was taught into my spiritual practice. To achieve my new aim, I initially studied for a certificate, followed by a diploma in life coaching. This proved to be an amazing experience. Not only was I helping others to go forward, I was also going through a cleansing process myself. I learned how to master the self rather than the other way around.

All of this culminated in my moving forward in my life in 2006. Becoming a life coach helped me to understand my personal values, the rules that I choose to live by. Values are "habits of thought." They are picked up from our families, teachers, those in authority, and friends who have been part of our lives. These elements all help in shaping our values. Our values and beliefs affect what we think, say, and do. My personal ten main values, in no particular order, are

honesty
family
loyalty
compassion
self-discipline
respect
spirituality
peace
honor
love

Our values define who we are and what we do. They can change as we change. Something that may be important to us when we are young might become unimportant to us as adults. As a teenager, freedom may be the most important value, but a few years on, justice may become more important. For me, as a young adult, pride and independence were my main values, mainly because they came from my mother, a very proud and independent woman. Not all values and beliefs serve us well, and sometimes we may need to question our beliefs to see if the time has come to change our habit of thought and look at what is important to us now. Some values are referred to as core values; these are the ones that are relevant to the majority of areas of our lives. For example, if we were to hold a deep conviction of, say, religion then this is likely to be a core value in our life.

Take some time out now, armed with pen and paper, and think about what is most important to you. List as many values you can think of that shape your life.

Make four columns of around ten values, listing them in order of importance. For example, if security is the most important value in your life right now, then put security at the top of your first list.

Continue, list by list, until you have at least forty values written down.

Now, take another sheet of blank paper and look at your values. If you need to shift a few around, just place a number beside them so, for instance, if power was in row four and the fifth word down, but now you think actually power is just as important as, say, security put a number two beside it.

On your other sheet of paper, take the first ten values, one by one, and ask yourself why each value is so important to you. Use your pen and paper to write down your answer to this question.

Example: Answer (1) Honesty is very important to me because my father always told me to be true to myself. I expect honesty from others so I can evaluate where I stand. By being honest with others, I allow them to know where they stand. (Yes, there are ways of being diplomatically honest, so I'm not saying that one needs to be blunt or rude, but by being honest will allow your life to run much more smoothly).

If we look at my sample statements, we can see that honesty was taught to me by my father, my father was important and loved by me, and being true to myself makes me feel comfortable within myself. Whether others are honest or not makes no difference to me; what makes the difference is my expectation of honesty from others and vice-versa.

I am honest with others because I believe that others expect honesty from me. I believe that the more we are dishonest, the more our subconscious mind becomes confused, and that's when we get ourselves into trouble. So for me, honesty will always be one of my core values.

Once you have written why your ten core values are important to you, think about which ones you will continue with and which ones you need to let go of. This technique was of great help to me when I was learning to become a coach; it allowed me to see what was really important to me at that moment in my life and gave me the chance to change habits and thoughts that were no longer empowering to me.

I find that one of the things we forget to do is to reward ourselves. It doesn't have to be an expensive treat or happen all of the time, but an occasional acknowledgement shows that you appreciate yourself. Here is a list of treats to indulge yourself with:

1. Take yourself to a movie or a play.
2. Book a long weekend away somewhere special.
3. Go on a course or workshop you have always wanted to do.
4. Buy yourself a bunch of beautiful flowers.
5. Book yourself a holistic treatment.
6. Book yourself a beauty treatment.
7. Enroll in a health club
8. Have what I call a "duvet day"—stay in bed all day and do nothing.
9. Book a hot air balloon ride.
10. Take a day trip around a city you know nothing about.

The list could be endless. But the point I'm trying to get across is that we need to show love to ourselves. This is not a selfish act but an act of self-empowerment.

Spiritual Keys

- *If you are considering starting a business in Reiki—or indeed any other field—please believe in yourself; anything is possible. Look into your mind's eye to see the things you want for your future.*
- *With regard to payment for treatments, people should not pay for healing but rather the time it takes you to give healing. We all have self–worth, and a Reiki treatment is worth something.*
- *As a healer, one needs to be careful that one has not taken on too much. If you feel that your energy is depleted, it's time to cut loose and focus on self. Heal yourself to become better placed to go back and continue to help others.*
- *Let go of whatever or whoever is not in harmony with your goals and achievements. Be happy in yourself, and take responsibility for your own happiness. If you rely on others to provide your happiness, somewhere along the line they will fail you.*
- *Do not allow other people to tell you something cannot be achieved. Many people refuse to take chances in business because they fear criticism from other people.*
- *Other people do not pay your bills or put food on your table.* You do!

Chapter Six

Personal Development

Coaching, Goal Setting, and Exercises

Continuing Professional Development (CPD) is a must for therapists who take their practice seriously. Through CPD, practitioners show that they are continually updating their healthcare education. For most professional organizations, CPD credit can be obtained in many ways, such as reading books, magazines, or articles that enhance your professional knowledge, carrying out research, or attending courses and workshops. One of the most important things about CPD is the evaluation that comes afterward. You can perform self-evaluation by asking yourself questions such as, "What did I learn from this?" or "What do I need to do now?" Reflecting upon these questions recording your answers is helpful. I personally try to keep on top of my CPD, and I am always looking for new ways to enhance my knowledge of Reiki and life coaching.

I became qualified as a personal life coach in 2004, which was not an easy task. As you read this chapter, you might want to have pen and paper handy, as I have compiled a few tips for you to make note of.

Life Coaching is a temporary relationship between two people: the coach and the person being coached. In my line of work, life coaching is also a holistic process that considers all parts of a client's life—mind, body, and spiritual aspects. There has to be absolute commitment from both parties. For me, this creates a bond of trust and ensures that the relationship can run smoothly.

When coaching a client, I'm always looking to see if the client is seeking new ways of doing things. I'm also listening to hear if they would prefer to talk about their problems rather than create solutions. My job would then be to encourage them to engage in action, after each session, by researching or sometimes even creating new behavior to help them move forward in achieving their goals. A good exercise that I find very beneficial when clients become stuck in creating action is getting them to list the benefits they will receive from taking any particular action toward their goal. By doing this exercise, they can focus on the benefits rather than the action.

Something I come across with many clients is a belief system or certain types of behaviors that do not serve them well. Once again, we would make a list of these beliefs or behaviors. We would then go through the list, asking the question, "What will your life look like in say five, ten, or maybe fifteen years if nothing changes in your beliefs or behaviors?" It's amazing to hear what comes to us in the answers to these types of questions when people are being honest. You may like to try it and see what you come up with.

This chapter on coaching is a good place to talk about dignity. Dignity is about showing self-respect and having balance and self–esteem. You will be surprised how much others will respect you when you show respect for yourself. We need to become solid in ourselves by not being particularly interested in what other people say or think. Instead, we need to become busy and focused in the pursuit of achieving our goals, Forget attention-seeking, show poise, have good manners, be polite and considerate to others, become courteous and charming, keep your promises and be civil. When greeting someone, instead of your usual hi or hello, why not say good morning, good afternoon, or good evening to start a conversation? Try to become someone that others might look up to—and yes, you can still relax and have lots of fun.

Goals

The nearest most of my clients have ever come to goal setting is on New Year's Eve, when they promise themselves that they are going to give up smoking, get trim for the summer, or write a book. The problem is, most people never actually get around to keeping these promises. Often, people come to see me because they have come to realize that they need help with making goals and sticking to them.

The first question I always ask is what exactly the client wants to achieve. Knowing what you really want is the first step. The next step is to determine if your goals are achievable. For clients who have several goals, we need to determine which goals are short term and which are long term by ranking the goals in priority order. Goals need to be put into context—the what, where, when, and with whom they can be pursued must be defined.

This brings me to action, as without action there can be no change. Talking action is the easy part; the actual doing of action is where most people stop. For me personally this is when my determination and persistence kicks in. For my clients, this is the bit I love the most—motivating them into taking action. To be honest, some of my clients will tell you that I am quite scary when I motivate, but they would not have it any other way, as they do understand that I have their best interests at heart. Motivation is the fuel that turns a thought into action. It's like giving the clients a kick-start that gets them going.

I hope you have your pen and paper ready because here goes. Goals should be written down. By writing your goals down, you begin to realize that you are committed to making them real. The next important thing when writing your goals is to write them in the present tense your subconscious mind works better when the instructions you give it are positive and in the present tense. For example, my goal for writing this book went like this: "I am writing a book about becoming inspired by Reiki energy" rather than "I want to write a book about Reiki."

Here are some questions that may help you write down your goals. Write down as many goals as you can think of, then look at each goal and determine the following:

1. What information will I need to make this goal a reality?
2. What stands in my way of achieving this goal?
3. What resources will I need to help me achieve this goal?
4. What are the first steps I can take toward the achievement of this goal?
5. What will happen if I don't take action toward the achievement of my goal?

Once you have written down your goals, it is important to review them as often as possible. I had read somewhere that the ideal times for reviewing are first thing in the morning and last thing at night. To remind myself of my goal, I got some plain paper and I wrote, "I'm a successful author" in capital letters on several sheets. I stuck these sheets all over my bedroom. One was on the ceiling above my bed, so as soon as I opened my eyes I, would see it. Others were on each wall. No matter which way I turned, I would see it. I even posted one on my glass shower door. If you don't believe me, try it yourself.

Next, don't forget to reward yourself when you achieve goals, whether they are large or small. By rewarding yourself, you stimulate your enthusiasm to create more goals. A reward can be anything from buying yourself a treat or going to see a movie to booking a long weekend away somewhere special or attending a course or workshop you have always wanted to attend. Something else that will help is creating a success notebook. Write everything you have ever accomplished in it—the longer the list, the more you will want to accomplish.

Now, if you decide that what you want out of life is to create strong relationships with others, I have a list of some ways to help you achieve this:

1. Always greet people with a smile.
2. Offer help to others when you have some spare time.
3. Share positive information books, CDs, DVDs, or anything you feel a friend or relative may benefit from.
4. Send hello and thank-you notes just to make someone you know smile.
5. Call people you know and tell them how much you appreciate them; leave a message if you have to.
6. Take a friend out for lunch or dinner and give him or her your undivided attention.
7. Try hard not to get involved in negative gossip.
8. Always find ways to enhance others' self-esteem.
9. Give others the benefit of doubt; try not to pre-judge.
10. Praise others when praise is due.
11. Give and receive lots of hugs.
12. Occasionally put yourself in others' shoes. If you feel that something hurts you, it probably hurts the other person too.
13. Always try to encourage others positively.
14. Buy or lend someone you care about a copy of this book.

Goal setting is essential to becoming successful in any field. You need to make goal setting part of your purpose, and you need to put your heart and soul into it. Once you have set a goal, you need to take action. It is a good idea to take some sort of action within twenty-four hours of setting your goals, as it will send a message of commitment to the universe and start the ball rolling, so to speak. Don't make a goal a wish or a hazy dream. Make it an objective. Nothing, and I mean nothing, will happen if you don't take action and the necessary steps forward. Without goals, we would just wander through life with no real purpose in mind. Get a clear, undiluted focus of where you want to go and what you want to do in life; have great intentions for yourself. Ask yourself where you want to be in five years, ten years, or even fifteen years.

Don't leave your future to chance. Form images in your mind's eye of where you want to be. If you have no agenda or plans, you will accomplish absolutely nothing. Forget about what kind of background or education you had and focus on now. Don't just say that you want a good job or to travel the world—describe the job, describe how you will travel, down to the last detail. Plan ahead, visualize it. Having your heart set on a specific goal will provide you with enough energy to achieve what you are aiming for. Become obsessed, and let no one stand in your way; become ruthless and determined to see your goal through to the end. Put persistence in your pocket and run with it. The principle of persistence is to follow your goal through from beginning to end; the lack of persistence will not carry you to where you want to go.

With will power and effort to succeed, persistence will come naturally. When you know that things may be getting you down, go back to the reason why you decided to achieve your goal in the first place and think about what would happen if you decided not to continue in pursuit of that goal. Think back and acknowledge any goals you have already achieved. This alone should give you the energy you need to get back up and focus. Don't accept defeat. If one way is not working, then find another way or sit quietly and ask the universe for guidance.

Think of famous people like Nelson Mandela, who used his faith in God to create persistence. Laziness and persistence do not go together. Not making excuses or giving up builds persistence. In my treatment room, I have three framed posters on the wall. One says "Goals," another says "Make it happen," and the third one says "Persistence." Once you have an idea, the desire, trust, and faith within yourself, persistence will ride with you all the way to the end.

I first understood persistence many years ago when I read the autobiography, *Losing My Virginity* by Sir Richard Branson. Branson mentions the time when his school headmaster's parting words were, "Congratulations, Branson. I predict that you will either go to prison or become a millionaire."

Well, you get no brownie points for guessing which road Branson ended up on. If I ever get a chance to meet him, I will have to ask the question, "Did your head teacher's comments contribute to your desire, determination, and persistence in becoming a millionaire?"

Your goals are your future. If we were to look at our present and give clear decisive instructions to our mind about our goals for the future, when we get to that specific time in our life, we'll find that those goals have been realized, provided that we have done the things that needed to be done in order to achieve them. We need to understand that whatever we are experiencing in our lives today is what we have thought about in our past, whether this was yesterday, last week, or even last year. As we think about being happy and expecting happiness for our future, we begin to start the creative process toward happiness.

Here are some ways to keep yourself focused on accomplishing your goals and building positive habits.

1. Deposit and withdraw positive thoughts only.
2. Plan tomorrow's work today.
3. Read lots of self-help and inspirational books.
4. Use setbacks as lessons, and learn from them.
5. Leave negative language alone.
6. Rest if you must, but do not quit.

My father had a saying: "If you don't have anything good to say, then don't say anything at all"

When thinking and talking about your goals, always think and talk positively. Try not to be one who looks back on life and regrets all the missed opportunities. By setting goals, you will get a clear vision of where you are going. Share your goals only with people who set goals too; not everyone will be happy to share your enthusiasm for success. Be optimistic, and allow yourself to believe everything and anything is possible. People sometimes ask me how I can remain so upbeat and positive all of the time, no matter what else is going on in my. Here's how:

1. Spend more time with optimistic and enthusiastic people, as you will rub off each other. It's important to spend quality time with the right people; pessimistic people can drain you if you allow them to.
2. Don't allow other people to milk your confidence. That is what I call adult bullying. Stand up for yourself.
3. Be genuinely honest and truthful with yourself.
4. Make a list of empowering beliefs. Start by telling yourself that you are happy from within.

5. Choose the type of positive person you want to be right here, right now.
6. Never be afraid to declare your love freely and frequently to the people who are close to you. The more love you give, the more you will receive.
7. Life is full of problems. I am yet to meet anyone who has escaped life's problems. For this reason, we need to find ways to solve our problems. Try not to blame yourself for any negative things that you have done in the past. Accept what has been done and forgive yourself. Self-forgiveness is a good, healing process. Stand in front of a mirror, which will increase your power, and repeatedly say,

   I will forgive myself and others more easily.

   I will tune into an infinite source of guidance and energy.

   I will treat myself more lovingly.

   I will be more patient with myself.

   I will acknowledge my connection to this wonderful universe.

   I will control my own power and make my own decisions.

   I will release and let go of any anger.

   I will release and let go of the past.

   I will take responsibility for my own personal wellness.

   I will love myself unconditionally.

   I will feel compassion for all living beings.

   I will be happy, fulfilled, and content.

It does not matter if the words are not the same; simply use words that empower you. Set goals that will make you do things. Take a pen and some paper, now. At the top of the paper, write in capital letters I AM FOCUSED ON [This can be anything].

List three main things that are a priority for you at this moment in time. Now, put this list somewhere that you will automatically see it at least three times a day. If you working outside of home, make a copy and take it with you. Just make sure you see this list first thing in the morning, once during the day, and last thing at night.

I suggest three goals so you won't get sidetracked or confused by focusing on too many things.

Now, get rid of clutter—all of your outdated bits and pieces, including emotional clutter. You need to make clear space for the new energy that is ready to come into your life. If something or someone does not serve you well, get rid of it. Look at your life, and ask yourself the question, "What would my life look like if it was perfect in every way? Your job is to now create that picture.

Here is a quick visualization process you can use.

Relax and close your eyes. Summon up a golden broom in your hand. You are going to use this golden broom to sweep out all the things you no longer want in your life. See yourself sweeping with your golden broom. What you are discarding could be debt, people, bad situations, even bad health. That's it; just spend a few minutes sweeping it all out. Now find yourself a dustbin that will fit what is being thrown out. Take the lid off and place this clutter in the bin. Close the lid, and, with a smile and sigh of relief, now see yourself turning your back on the dustbin and walking away from it. Open your eyes and carry on with the rest of your day feeling cleansed and refreshed.

You would be surprised how powerful this process can be. The more you do it, the more your subconscious mind will accept it as truth and help you to find ways to get rid of clutter. Never place your power outside of yourself; use the power that lies within you to create the life you desire. It is your birthright to be happy. Do not allow any limiting beliefs to stop you from creating what you want or taking you where you want to go in life. Try not to become desperate; all that does is push away the positive outcomes.

Spiritual Keys

- *In life coaching, there is no such thing as failure. Failure is only the individual's own interpretation of any given situation.*
- *As a life coach, I must have absolute clarity about what the goal is that my client wants.*
- *I must encourage my clients to develop that same clarity for their goals.*
- *A coaching process consists of dealing with each goal in turn, before moving on to anything else.*
- *Try not to aim too low in life; failure to think big may hold you back.*

Chapter Seven

Dream Weaver

Visualization, Manifestation, and Feelings

I have used the word "visualize" in previous chapters; here I would like to explain in depth how I see and use visualization. I believe that we are all blessed with innate imaginative powers, and as children, we use these powers without fear. As we get older, the majority of us lose our ability to use our imagination because we are taught that it is "unscientific" and "illogical."

We do not all perceive the world in the same way, and it was not until late in my adult life that I realized this. The thought processes we use are sometimes visual—the ability to see pictures in our minds—while some of us are more auditory and perceive the world through sound and words. Others interpret through emotions, which is called kinesthetic. I should not leave out the olfactory system, which covers our smell and taste. Many animals use the olfactory system to hunt for food. When visualizing, it is possible to use a combination of these systems.

Let me give you a personal example. When I take time out to visualize and create an image in my mind, not only do I see the image but I am able to add sound to it. If, for example, I visualize myself on a beautiful beach, I can see the sand and the sea, and I am able to hear the sound of the water. If visualizing an oriental lily, I would also smell the sweet perfume. All this takes practice, so don't be too hard on yourself if it does not happen straight away.

I have met many people over the years who find it hard to see pictures. For these people, if I were to say the word "horse" to them, they would see the word "horse," not a picture of a horse. It is possible to enhance the skill of visualization by practicing seeing pictures. Listening to guided meditations on tape or CD can help with this. Recordings of this kind are designed to take listeners on a journey where they are encouraged to use their conscious mind—seeing, feeling, or listening—and at the same time, allow the unconscious mind to work on inner qualities such as greater self-awareness or inner calm. I would like to point out that these recordings are designed for complete relaxation, so they should not be used while driving or when using machinery.

When I teach a Reiki course, regardless of the level, I always use guided meditation at least once. The reason is that this is a simple way of introducing the subject of visualization to those who have never had the opportunity to experience it before. It is rewarding for me to hear the feedback, once we have all listened and practiced.

Visualization can be used in other areas of our lives, such as being successful at sports. Take sprinter Usain Bolt of Jamaica, for instance. He won the men's one-hundred-meter finals at the 2008 Olympics held in Beijing. He won the race in 9.69 seconds, beating the world record. What an achievement! I wonder how much visualization went into Usain winning that race?

See yourself, feel yourself, or hear yourself becoming a winner. If there is only one trophy or prize, believe that you are the one who will receive it—and it will be yours.

Visualization can help in other areas as well. Let's look at shyness, for example. Many people believe that shyness cannot be eliminated. I can tell you that this is absolutely not true. I have personally helped others to get over their shyness by using the power of visualization. It has helped them change the way they think about themselves and their shyness by changing their thoughts of how other people see or think about them. Using guided meditation, coupled with visualization, I would ask them to see themselves as they wanted to be seen and how they would want other people to see them. I would then ask them to practice until they began to believe that it was working. We've witnessed some great results.

Looking into the future, I would love to believe that one day visualization would be taught in schools, to our children. I firmly believe that if we introduced life coaching skills at secondary or high school level and used methods of positive action, that the current climate of violence and crime that is sweeping through our inner cities could be curbed. We could teach youngsters that there is a better way. Creative visualization could be used as a means of improving performance in any given goal.

Manifestation

This is a difficult area to write about because many people are skeptical about the subject. I have had people say to me that it is not possible to make something appear at will just by thinking about it. I would answer this by saying there is a lot more to the process than just thinking and receiving.

Manifestation is something we experience in our lives every day. First we need to understand how we get what is manifested in our lives. We also need to understand that the thoughts and emotions we manifest in our lives are the same thoughts and emotions that we give our attention to. For example, if we are experiencing happiness in our lives and we focus on being happy and joyful, we will create more happiness and joy—rather than the opposite state.

Each day I spend some time on my own thinking about my future and how I see myself in the future. By using visualization, I can bring forth all the things I want to see for my future. As I step forward into the future—which may be a day, a month, or even a year from the time when my thoughts are first created, I find that my thoughts manifest into reality. I know that for some people this will be unbelievable, but I speak from life experience. If I can help it, I do not allow thoughts of a negative nature to enter my mind.

When clients come to see me because they want change in their lives, my aim is to let them see that they need to focus on what it is that they really want. If, for example, they are overweight, I encourage them to see themselves slim rather than focusing on how they see themselves now. I encourage them to, tell themselves that they have a perfect figure. You may wonder how you can tell yourself a lie. But the subconscious mind needs repetitive affirmation that something is true before the concept can become a reality. It will, of course, be difficult at first because all you will see is what is in front of you. If you believe and continue to focus your thoughts on that vision of yourself as slim, your subconscious mind will act, doing what is needed to create that reality. You will be guided in thought and action to the achievement of your goal. All you need to add is persistence and determination. Try keeping this experience to yourself to ward off any negative influences. Spend time each day, twenty or thirty minutes, focusing on the positive thoughts of what you want to achieve and see in your future. Provided that you have not allowed doubts to cloud your mind along the way, your thoughts will eventually manifest into reality.

Feelings

Our thoughts also control how we feel. Think about it—things might not be going the way we would like them to at any specific time in our lives, but the only person who can control how we feel as individuals is us!

Allowing other people to create our happiness is not always a good thing; if they let us down, we end up feeling bad. Feeling good should be a daily goal, a birthright. Feeling good eliminates stress within the body. There are so many ways to create good feelings—do things we enjoy, take up a hobby, listen or dance to some music, go for a good long walk, spend time with friends, family, and people we love. Being around people who make us laugh and feel grateful provides positive energy; the energy of gratitude is one of the most powerful energies we can experience.

Sometimes all it will take for you to get yourself in a joyous mood is to smile. Try it now: smile and feel the difference in your body. Do things to make others smile—send a joke, send a card. Show appreciation to those around you by making others joyful, and in return, you will create joy for yourself. A word of warning, and this is not to scare you, but try hard not to give away your personal power. Don't allow others to drain your good feelings and energy; stand up for yourself and take control of your life. If you are feeling good, you will think good things; if you're feeling bad, you will think bad things. Life is a physical manifestation of thoughts and feelings that occupy our minds and bodies.

The only thing that will stop you from realizing your goals is a subconscious belief that you cannot. I believe that we need to learn to question our thoughts. Simply having a thought doesn't mean that the thought is true! The way you feel will be your indicator of how you create or manifest the outcome of your life. Try to remember a time when you had real happiness. Go back to that memory and remember as many details of what you felt within and tell yourself that this is the way you would like to feel for the rest of your life, no matter what situations you may find yourself in. You may still have bad days, but the more you can tell yourself that you're feeling good, the more you will feel good.

Our thoughts, feelings, and actions are all made up of energy, and it is up to us as individuals to take responsibility for the way that we feel and to create more positive energy within and around our own energy field. Our feelings are very powerful, and I believe that we get what we feel rather than what we say. In other words, even if our words are positive, if we are in a place of feeling bad, then it is not necessarily possible to create or manifest what it is that we want. For example, if you are looking for a new job and you say to yourself *I would like to get a new job*, but, at the same time, your subconscious mind is saying *why bother? You won't get it; you never do,* well it's that subconscious thought that will manifest into reality.

What is important is to align our conscious minds and our subconscious minds. Both have to be thinking positive thoughts. It's no use telling yourself that you are going to do something when you know, deep down, that you are not. That is not to say that you cannot trick your subconscious mind into believing something, however that will only work if you mean it and give your subconscious mind consistent, repetitive thoughts of what it is that you would like to create. Feel the feeling of being happy as often as you can, and eventually your subconscious mind will believe it too. Get your mind relaxed and into a calm state so that you can visualize the thoughts that you want to create.

Here is a guided meditation to help you to relax and create calm. This is for when you're having one of those days when everything seems so uphill and you're not quite sure where to turn.

Find an upright chair to sit in or sit on the floor with your legs crossed. Keep your spine as straight as possible with your neck stretched a little and your chin slightly tilted toward your chest. Keep your shoulders relaxed at all times.

Close your eyes and focus on your breathing. Don't change the pattern of your breathing, just continue to breathe normally.

Now see in your mind's eye a bright royal-blue beam of light coming through the top of your head. This beam of light is glowing through your whole body, and there is nothing for you to do but sit and absorb this beautiful beam of light. Just stay with it, letting go of any unwanted thoughts and letting go of any tension you may be feeling.

Just sit and bathe yourself in this beautiful beam of light. When you are ready, allow this light to take your burdens, worries, or fears. Give everything that is wearing you down to this beautiful beam of light. Once you have done that, the beautiful beam of light has a gift for you. It's a gift of strength. Feel the gift of strength that has been given to you. Now take this strength and thank your beam of light for its gift. Continue to focus on your breathing.

Now you will see this light disappear from your whole body through the base of your feet. In its place comes an emerald-green beam of light. It enters through the top of your head. This beam of light is glowing through your whole body.

Once again, there is nothing for you to do but sit and absorb this beautiful beam of light. Just stay with it, letting go of any unwanted thoughts, letting go of any stress, anxiety, or heartache. Give everything that is grinding you down to this beautiful beam of light.

Once you have done that, the beautiful beam of light has another gift for you. This time, it's a gift of love, and it's all for you. Feel your gift of love. Now take that love and thank your beam of light for its gift. Continue to focus on your breathing.

Now see this light disappear from your whole body through the base of your feet.

In comes a bright white beam of light coming, entering through the top of your head. This beam of light is glowing through your whole body and there is nothing for you to do but sit and soak up this beautiful beam of light. When you're ready, allow this light to take any anger, sorrow, or regrets you have. Give everything that is keeping you down to this beautiful beam of light.

Once you have done that, the beautiful beam of light has a gift for you. It's a gift of peace, and it's all for you. Feel the gift of peace that has been given to you. Now take your gift of peace and thank your beam of light for its gift. Continue with your breathing.

Now, in your mind, count backward from ten to one. Then open your eyes.

You can do these exercises at your desk during your lunch break or in your garden. In fact, you can do them anywhere that you will not be disturbed. It may look long, but once you read through it a couple times and practice it, you will see that it can take only as long as you want it to.

Strength, love, and peace carried me through some of the toughest times. Mainly because strength, love, and peace are included in my core values. I think that strength came from watching my mother working as hard as she did; the love echoes the love that she gave me, and the peace is what she carried with her. Now, I know we are human beings and we have emotions, which is quite natural. It is okay to sometimes feel anger, as long as we remain in control; it is okay if we cry from time to time, as we need to let these kinds of emotions out. Once they're out, we can deal with them and move on to being happy and joyful once again.

Spiritual Keys

- *Pause for a moment, now, in this present moment and consider things that you have done today or even yesterday—for example, consider the clothes that you are wearing. You thought about them and visualized them in your mind's eye before you put them on.*
- *You may have made a cup of tea today; this requires that you think about putting the kettle on to boil. You would probably have said in your mind at the same time, "I must put that kettle on," probably without even hearing yourself saying it.*
- *Always have a positive picture of yourself. Picture yourself successful. Visualize the person you would like to become. See yourself as confident. Always see yourself attracting the people who are in harmony with your current intentions.*
- *Always see yourself in a world that is full of abundance, and recognize that there is no limit to the abundance that our universe has to offer. As individuals, we create our own world, and we should allow others to create theirs too.*
- *Feel good as often as you can for as long as you can.*
- *Tell yourself each morning that you feel that today is going to be a good day.*

Chapter Eight

If Ye Have Faith

Affirmations, Gratitude, and Prayer

A positive affirmation is a phrase or thought that can be used to change our beliefs. How and what we think affects the way we are and how we see ourselves. We can use the principle of affirmations for the purpose of giving orders to our subconscious mind. They can be used to learn new patterns of thoughts and discard old patterns of thought that no longer serve us well. We can write, speak, sing, or even chant an affirmation.

Although I have been using affirmations for many years—certainly before my Reiki existence—as my father taught me, it was my friend Maureen who came to my rescue (once again) and put a name to what I had been doing. I used to call it using positive statements. I have now, with experience, come to realize that affirmations work best if you mix faith and emotion while saying the words. Amazingly, I have found that sometimes affirmations will happen instantly, while at other times they can take what seems like a lifetime to manifest.

Let me give you an example from my own experience. A few years ago, we planned a trip to Australia over the Christmas and New Year period. We spent the first week in Cairns, and from there, we went on to Brisbane to spend Christmas with family. We planned to spend the New Year with some good friends of mine, celebrating New Year's Eve at Sydney Harbor with thousands of other people.

Having broken our journey in Hong Kong, we continued to Australia. On the plane, I was reading a book called *Feel the Fear and Do It Anyway* by Susan Jeffers, and I remember that she mentioned something about index cards and positive quotes. At that moment, I started to say repeatedly to myself, *I use affirmation cards every day*. I said it over and over in my mind until I believed it.

We arrived in Sydney, spent an evening, and, the following day, we headed off by plane up to Cairns. Once we were settled in the hotel, I decided to go off and do some sightseeing. As I walked down the road, I was strongly drawn to a particular shop. This shop was full of crystals, gift cards, and candles, as well as many other items. There was no one else in the shop apart from the assistant, and I began to look around. Within seconds, I looked down, and there on the shelf was a box that read *I Can Do It Cards* by Louise L Hay, the author of *You Can Heal Your Life.* I quickly opened the box. Unbelievably, I found a sixty-card pack of positive affirmations.

I turned around to go and pay for the cards, and I noticed that there were eight other people looking around the shop. At the cash desk the assistant said, "Thank You."

I looked behind me, as I did not realize that she was addressing me. I looked at her quizzically, and she said, "Thank you" a second time. She then added, "For bringing all these people into my shop. You must have an enormous amount of positive energy surrounding you."

I smiled and thanked her, paid for my cards, and left.

Now this was a true-life experience. I'm not saying it will happen like this all of the time, but believe me, affirmations do work. The two following affirmations have been of benefit to me, and have had an extraordinarily positive influence on my life.

Limitations are merely opportunities to grow. I use them as stepping-stones to successes.

I am ready to be healed. I am willing to forgive. All is well.

The first quote reminds me of all the obstacles I have overcome to get to where I am now. The latter reminds me of my passion for Reiki and how I came to be inspired by Reiki energy. It also reminds me of how continuous self-healing has allowed me to forgive and let go of the past, so that I could receive peace of mind and harmony in my life.

My sincere thanks to Louise L Hay and her *I Can Do It Cards.*

Our thoughts are projected into the universe as vibrations. Vibrations can carry good intentions or bad intentions; the choice is always yours. Choose good thoughts; choose positive affirmations.

I have listed some positive affirmations here. Feel free to make them your own, or see if you can make some up for yourself.

- I am worthy.
- I am deserving.
- I am loved.
- I am gifted.
- I am special.
- I am beautiful.
- I am ready to receive.
- I am ready to release my limitations.
- I am ready to live well.
- I am ready to love.
- I am attracting happiness and joy into my life.
- I am grateful for each gift I receive in my life.
- I am full of light and radiate success.
- I am full of abundance, which flows through me.

- I am healthy and full of energy.
- I am moving through life without resistance.
- I am attracting only those who are in harmony with me.
- I am a magnet that only attracts what is good.
- I am at peace.

Through constant affirmations, instructions are given to our subconscious mind, which, in turn, helps us to achieve our goals. It is one of the most powerful ways to create a vibrational match between ourselves and the universe and to attract the happiness we are searching for.

Once you have created your affirmations, try to use them daily. I usually say my affirmations to myself in the pool as I swim each length. This stops me from cluttering up my mind. Having said that, it is best to say them out loud with feeling, so that you can experience the emotions that they evoke and increase your desire to act on the reality of your words. So remember, as you say your affirmations, that for them to reach your subconscious mind, you have to believe them. This is the only way to achieve desirable results. If you get the principle of affirmations right, you will be able to focus and concentrate on a particular goal and your burning desire to make that goal a reality.

As I said earlier, affirmations can be written down. Take a piece of paper. At the top, write what you would like to achieve. Next, write why you would like to achieve this particular goal. Finally, write the reasons why you think you will achieve this.

It may go something like this:

I would like to be happy and joyful every day of my life.

By being happy and joyful, I will feel full of energy and in good health.

I believe I will achieve this state of happiness because it is my birthright; I expect it, and I deserve it.

This example is a short version, but your written affirmation can be as long or as short as you choose. Try doing some for yourself, and have fun creating as many affirmations as you can. Then, take one that stands out for you now. Repeat it at least three times a day, with positive emotions, for the next thirty days. This will allow your subconscious to absorb the information. Then watch to see the difference it makes in your life.

Gratitude

For me, giving gratitude is the most powerful exercise anyone can practice. As soon as I take my first breath each morning, sometimes before even opening my eyes, I say the words, "Thank you. Then, through the course of each day, I am constantly giving thanks for all kinds of things, and I do not mean only material things.

Let me take you through a typical grateful day. When I look out my bedroom window each morning, I thank the universe for the ponds in my garden, for the water that runs freely so the fish may swim. I'm thankful for the trees that surround my home and for the different shades of green that they bring. When I hear the birds singing, I give thanks once again that I have the ears to listen to such beauty.

I give thanks for the clothes I wear, the food I eat, for the people I have met in my life and share laughter or sadness with. The list is endless. One might ask how I find the time. The answer is simply that gratitude is not prayer. It is giving of thanks in the same way that you would say thank you to someone for giving you good service. With gratitude, you are thanking the universe or God for all creation.

Even now, I am giving thanks for the time I have been granted to enable me to put my thoughts on paper so that I can share my experience with others.

If you do not already do so, start right now giving thanks. You could give thanks that you have the eyes to read this book.

The more thanks you give, the more the universe will give to you. The more you believe you deserve and ask for, the more you shall have. We should also give thanks for our problems and setbacks in life, as they, too, are gifts that help us look for solutions. Trust me; it is true.

What we need to understand is that, once we have been blessed or fortunate to receive the gifts that we have asked for, we sometimes forget that we need to acknowledge that blessing or gift with gratitude. The more we give thanks, the more we will receive. I cannot stress this enough. Our mental attitude needs to change, moving toward gratitude by allowing our thoughts of gratefulness to bring us closer to the creative energy of the universe. We must always give thanks for everything that we receive. Gratitude is what connects us to the universe and its power. We can all start by stopping the constant complaining of our shortcomings; being grateful will move us in the direction of everything that is good, and it will bring us closer to whatever it is we all desire.

When we receive things such as nature, sunshine, snow, and rain—all the things we take for granted, including birthday and Christmas presents—where do we really think they all come from? Who makes it all possible? Who allows the sun to shine and the snow and rain to fall? And when we are bought gifts and presents, where does the money come from? Who created the work to earn the money? Who gave the idea to whoever created the work?

I can tell you now that whoever or whatever created this universe, that is who we need to give thanks to on a regular basis.

Look at it from a biblical perspective. Jesus was always thanking his father for listening to him—something we as humans rarely do. When your children come with all their troubles and woes, at the end of the conversation do they ever say, "Oh, and by the way, thanks for listening"?

Listening is an act of giving. When others listen to us, we need to thank them for hearing us—just the same as Jesus did to his father. Our power in receiving lies in giving thanks. When we forget to give thanks or show gratitude, we lose the power to receive more good things. When we are in a state of appreciation, we become connected to pure positive energy. We will always go through times when we will look at our lives and think that nothing is going right. This is the time to look at what *is* going right and give thanks! Make giving thanks a way of life for you.

Prayer

I remember, from my childhood, vicars, ministers, and my father saying that everyone should have faith. None of them ever explained exactly what faith was or what it means to have faith. As I grew, my faith in God grew, and it is as strong today as it has ever been. At this point, I would like to explain that the word "God" is only a label for me, and you can use whatever name you please, be it Higher-self, Universe, Jah, or even Jehovah—anything you like. It all means the same thing. Don't allow the word "God" to frighten you.

There is a quote in the Bible: "I can do all things through Christ, which strengtheneth me." Philippians 4:13. For me, faith is a very positive and powerful experience. It is a state of mind that can be induced by affirmation or repeated self-talk that travels to the subconscious mind. The subconscious starts to believe what it is given, and when we mix belief with positive emotion, that is when our prayers are answered. If we can sincerely thank God for the things that we would like to create and believe in our imagination, before it becomes a reality, then that is what I call faith.

When I was growing up, if someone asked me if I was religious, I would have said yes. (Now I have let go of religion and embraced God instead.) This was mainly because my father was a deacon and I took on other people's beliefs, for example the idea that God exists outside of oneself. I used to think that God was a man who sat up high in the clouds watching everyone, making sure that everyone obeyed the Ten Commandments and striking down dead those who did not. I have now grown to believe that there is one supreme dynamic force that governs the universe—an unseen power that vibrates everywhere.

Now, I like to think of myself as spiritual. There is no man up in the sky who will stop loving us because we do not live up to other people's expectations. My personal belief is that God lives within and around us all. Maybe God and the universe is one and the same thing. Who really knows? We need to pause for a moment to consider the gifts that have been given to us by God, and in that same moment, recognize his presence in our lives.

A lot of the time, we misunderstand God, even when we think we understand. But when things go wrong in our lives, we sometimes ask *where is God now?* We feel abandoned when we need God most. We ask, *Where have you loved us?*

Believe me when I tell you that God always loves us, no matter what. Sometimes I think that God just wants us to grow up and understand that he or she should not have to prove to us all the time that we are loved; we just need to believe. For those who are still not quite sure about this God thing, just remember the next time you take a breath—that is all the proof you should need that God exists.

Over the years, when clients have asked me why God allows bad things to happen in the world, my answer is always that it is because God loves us and doesn't want to interfere with our freedom of choice. God is not asking us to obey, but rather to love.

Whenever I need answers to questions, I find them by going inside myself through solitude and silence. I might ask a particular question, then, while I go about my daily business, the answer will just come to me. I think this happens because of my faith and trust in both myself the universe.

Prayer can consist of absolutely anything—from giving thanks to asking for help or guidance in something you may be doing. We can pray for people who are in poor health, for happiness, or just for contentment. We can also do what I call a "hand over." Many years ago, a friend once asked me the question, "How do you sleep so soundly when you have so many troubles?"

The truth is, and this was my answer—I "hand it over" to the Lord. I ask him to look after my troubles while I sleep, knowing that I will collect them in the morning. By handing your worries over, you are left with a clear mind to go to sleep; your worries will be there for you in the morning. Having a good night's sleep will give you more energy to deal with your worries while you are awake.

Over the years, I have seen people kneel to pray, and I kneel most of the time too. However, I do not believe kneeling to pray is absolutely necessary. You may wish to stand or sometimes even simply bow your head. The bowing of the head, for me, shows respect, humbleness, and the seriousness of what it is I am praying for. Some people have special places where they pray—in church at a temple or shrine. Other people have a preference for praying indoors and some outside. The important thing to remember is that we can pray at any time, and our prayers are answered, wherever and whenever we pray. Praying is not about being religious. God and religion are two separate things.

For me, religion is a way, and God is the way. With praying comes relief from suffering and anxieties. Sharing your problems with God can bring tremendous comfort and relief from stress. Prayer time, just like sleeping and eating, needs to take place during a quiet time.

This is certainly the case for me. For those of you who say you don't have time to pray, I say, look at your life now and find something less important that you do and swap it for prayer time. Although I have said we can pray anywhere, it is lovely to have a special place dedicated to it, a sanctuary—a place where you can shut a door and keep the outside world at bay. This place can be anywhere, for example the bathroom, the kitchen, or even the garden shed. When you find it and go to that special place, you will never be alone. The one who answers your prayers will be there too. Please remember that these are only suggestions; you can do what feels right for you.

When you pray, believe that whatever you ask for will be received. If there's no belief, don't be surprised if your prayers do not materialize. When saying your prayers, you must be coherent, and you need to be definite about what it is you really want. Take time today to be in a place where you can be still, where you can know and accept the presence of God.

The following words come from a beautiful song that was written by my friend Derek. I would like to share it with you, as it sums up the kind of relationship I have with God:

> Would you want to talk with me, Lord
> Would you want to talk with me
> Would you come and talk with me, Lord
> Will you come and talk with me
>
> Eternal God
> Oh Savior King
> Eternal hope for every spring
> Eternal life is what you bring
> Eternal love
> Oh Heaven's King

Will you purify my soul, Lord
Would you want to talk with me
Cleanse and purify my soul, Lord
Will you come and talk with me
I know it's really you, Lord
Will you want to talk with me
I am listening for your voice, Lord
Will you come and talk with me

My Lord my God
Oh Savior king
Eternal joy forever spring
Eternal rest is what you bring
Eternal love
Oh Heaven's King

Come and fill me with that spirit
Will you come and talk with me
Come and fill me with that love, Lord
Will you come and talk with me
With the love that floods my yearnings
Will you come and talk with me
With a power that discerns me
Will you come and talk with me

Beginning end
Oh Savior King
Eternal peace for every spring
Eternal life is what you bring
Eternal love
Oh Heaven's King

As a friend that never leaves me
Will you come and talk with me

With correction that will guide me
Will you come and talk with me
Love has waited through the dry years
That are barren, filled with fear
Is it true that you are waiting
And you want to talk with me

Life giving love
Oh Savior King
Eternal hope for every spring
Eternal life is what you bring
Eternal love
Oh Heaven's King

Reiki is not a religion; it is universal energy, which is here for everyone and flows through all living things. When it comes to Reiki, there is nothing whatsoever to fear. Fear is something we all feel; don't for a minute think that you are the only person in the world who suffers from fear. We all feel fear at some stage in our lives.

People create fear for so many different reasons. I have found that it usually stems from the unknown. I have had many clients come to see me who are filled with fear of what others are saying about them. I try to help them put other people's opinions into perspective by asking if these other people contribute to paying their bills, putting food on their table, or keeping the roof over their heads. Nine times out of ten, the answer will be no. So, you see, other people will always have something to say (that we may not agree with), but there is no reason to fear what is being said.

The best way to deal with negative people is to listen if you must, thank them for what they have to say, and just ignore them.

They will eventually get the message when they see you haven't taken any notice. Never accept that others know what is best for you. Do listen to your own little voice that comes from within; trust and believe that little voice and greater wisdom will be yours. Try to have faith in your own perception of truth by accepting what the universe is trying to tell you; listen and trust. With faith, allow yourself to be opened up to greater wisdom.

Many years ago, my one and only fear was the fear of heights, something I never believed I would ever be cured of. Then I discovered this wonderful tool, Emotional Freedom Techniques. EFT was given to me in a workshop I attended. EFT is a simple tapping method based on ancient Chinese medicine. It uses energy pathways called meridians, just as acupuncture does. By tapping on key parts of our bodies, using only two fingers, we can balance our energy and clear any uncomfortable feelings—both emotional and physical. It is such a simple, yet very effective, method and it helped me to clear the unconscious conflict I had surrounding heights.

Another common fear clients come with is the fear of death. I sometimes wonder if the Buddhist theory of reincarnation may be of help. Sometimes I think that it might only cause confusion, because it would add the worry of what we would like to come back as. Now, because I get so many queries on the fear of death, I'm going to try to help you by letting you in on how I deal with it. For me, it's all about a mindset. I set in my mind that I can handle any given situation—even if, in reality, I cannot. But my mind has the belief that I should fear absolutely nothing and absolutely no one.

Over the years, I have developed trust in my ability through taking responsibility to handle whatever comes my way, no matter what. That includes my death. Sometimes I am asked whether I would fall apart if something happened to one of my children. My answer will always be if, God forbid, I had to lose one of my children through death, I would mourn just like anyone else. I have emotions too. But from the outset, I realize that death is the one thing we can all be sure of. I do go to church, and I do believe in God. However, I do not believe the saying in the bible "the Lord gave, and the Lord has taken away." For me, God does no such thing as taking us away from our loved ones. We go when we are meant to go because of so many different circumstances, even circumstances we sometimes can't explain. When it comes to children, my mindset is that they are needed in heaven too. I must say that I do find it a little harder for those who come to me for healing when they have lost their only child and are feeling pain. People don't like to remember or feel pain, but sometimes remembering is the only way to heal. To be honest, I find it easier to help those with other children left in the family to focus on.

A few years ago, my oldest sister, Charm, lost her youngest daughter, Leona, to sickle-cell anemia. Sickle cells tend to block blood flow, which causes pain, infection, and organ damage. The night Leona died, we were all gathered at the hospital. My sister Marva asked if there was something that I could do to help—with Reiki. I mentioned this to no one, not even Charm, as I didn't want to cause alarm. As I laid my hands on Leona, a little voice told me she was ready to go. I then asked the nurse if Leona would hear me if I spoke with her. "Oh, yes," replied the nurse. "She will hear you."

I bent down beside Leona's ear and whispered that I loved her and that she should look to the light, just keep looking to the light, and she would be guided. I was not quite sure where that insight came from, but I trusted it.

Four hours after I arrived home, I got the call to say that Leona had passed away. As the days went on, I tried to put myself in Charm's shoes, to help carry the pain. I'm not sure if that worked, as it was not my child but hers. I told her that I didn't know what to say to her, as I felt my words would not be enough. I decided just to be there for when or if she ever needed me.

Fear of anything brings worry, and if I am to be true to myself and my Reiki principle of "just for today, do not be worried," then carrying fear would only go against what I believe. Being true to ourselves makes life much easier; life only becomes complicated when we say one thing and our actions show the complete opposite. When we take fear away and start taking responsibility for our situations, life becomes much easier to deal with.

I would now like to share with you a beautiful poem written by Helen Steiner Rice:

> It's amazing and incredible,
> But it's as true as it can be
> God loves and understands us all
> And that means you and me.
> His grace is all-sufficient
> For both the young and old,
> For the lonely and the timid,
> For the brash and for the bold.
> His love knows no exceptions,
> So never feel excluded,
> No matter who or what you are
> Your name has been included.
> And no matter what your past has been,
> Trust God to understand,
> And no matter what your problem is
> Just place it in His Hand.
> For in all our unloveliness
> This great God loves us still,
> He loved us since the world began
> And what's more, He always will!

Spiritual Keys

- *If and when you pray, do it creatively. Your prayer is your affirmation to the God/Goddess within you. Picture your prayer; see your prayer coming true for you.*
- *Know that your God/Goddess is listening, and, most of all believe you have been heard.*
- *Give thanks that you have been heard; say, "Thank you for hearing me." Pray positively and never use negative words in you prayer. Remember to pray for others, and try hard not to go into prayer when you are worried or stressed.*
- *Worry is a state of mind based upon fear. Fear is negative and will play havoc on your body and mind.*
- *Always pray with a clear and open mind. Pray regularly; do not wait until there is a crisis in your life. Always stick to your purpose in life, and maintain your faith and gratitude.*
- *When you pray, have and hold steadfast faith. Your prayer will only fail if you begin to doubt or if you become uncertain and wavering in your thoughts.*

Chapter Nine

Universal Energies at Work

Japanese-Style Reiki

In the spring of 2006, we moved into our new home. I was due to get married that August, and family and friends were coming from all over the world. It was a very busy time. One day, as I sat at my desk, I felt drawn to a leaflet about the European Shinpiden, an advanced Reiki workshop. It would take place in September. As much as I would have loved to be involved, I felt that it was too soon after my wedding.

One year later, I was sifting through my mail when, lo and behold, I saw another leaflet: European Shinpiden dates for 2007. I looked at the possible dates and venues and saw that there would be a three-day session in Essex in October 2007. Still feeling a strong connection with Reiki, I e-mailed the organizer immediately, requesting more information regarding the course.

Shinpiden teachings, as taught by the International House of Reiki, focus on a traditional Japanese perspective of the system of Reiki. This course was to be led by Frans Steine. The name sounded familiar, so I went to my bookshelf—and there was the book I had read a few years earlier, *The Reiki Source Book,* by Bronwen and Frans Steine. Without even thinking about whether I could afford this, I knew immediately that I would attend. This was going to be an important part of my own personal Reiki development journey.

Bronwen and Frans Steine are internationally renowned Reiki authors, teachers, and researchers. Frans teaches regularly around the world and is the co-founder of the International House of Reiki, Australia. Frans is also co-author, with his wife Bronwen, of a number of books, including *The Japanese Art of Reiki, The Reiki Techniques Card Deck, The A–Z of Reiki,* and more recently, *Your Reiki Treatment.*

When I arrived at the venue in Munden, Essex, I walked into the room where everyone was having coffee, and I saw a tall, slim gentleman who immediately came toward me. I introduced myself to him and asked him who he was. He replied, "I am Frans Steine."

At that moment, I noticed Doreen Sawyer, the secretary of UK Reiki Federation, and I said to Frans that I would see him later. After greeting Doreen, I took my coffee and moved into the room where the course would take place. While I was browsing through the books that had been laid out on a table, it suddenly dawned on me who it was I had spoken to—Frans Steine.

Over the three days of the workshop, I studied and practiced the underlying, esoteric Japanese principles of the precepts, symbols, and mantras, including *reiju* (attunements). I also learned a unique method of working with the *jumon* (symbols) and mantras of the system, gaining a clearer understanding of what the system of Reiki is and where it came from. I learned about traditional Japanese philosophies and practice, such as the three diamonds of the Japanese energetic system, which helped me to feel more confident in my ability to teach Reiki to others.

Within the International House of Reiki, Bronwen and Frans teach three different levels of Reiki: Shoden, Okuden, and Shinpiden. Studying with International House of Reiki, I found my knowledge becoming a lot more transparent. One thing I had never noticed before was that the word "Reiki" was written with twenty-one *kanji* symbols. The word "Reiki" means "spiritual energy," and it had only recently been re-translated to "universal energy," or "universal life force energy" in the West. Shoden Reiki is very similar to first-degree Reiki; Okuden Reiki is similar to second–degree; and Shinpiden similar to third-degree Reiki—all without the extras and added confusion that I had been taught in the West. At the workshop, I found out that the five Reiki precepts, called *waka* in Japan, are used to develop spiritual and mental connection and were originally written by the Meiji emperor who ruled Japan from 1867–1912.

Earlier in this book, I described attunements. In Japan, this is called *reiju,* which means "spiritual blessings." Frans quite rightly explained that, in the West, the attunement process has become quite complex and confusing. In the West, *reiji* is given only during a Reiki course, whereas in Japanese teaching, it is given repeatedly at weekly or monthly meetings. It is said that each attunement received takes a person closer to realignment with the perfect function of the body—mentally, physically, emotionally, or spiritually. The changes are explained fully within the Shoden course.

The next thing that I noticed that was not included in my Western first-degree course was that we were encouraged to begin each day with fifteen minutes meditation. The meditation was provided in our manuals. We were then asked to keep a journal for twenty-one days to record all our thoughts and feelings. This was not taught in my Western Reiki courses.

Also at the Shinpiden course, I was told that, within the system of Reiki mantras and symbols, there are only four mantras and four symbols in traditional forms of Reiki. I had done all three Western Reiki levels, and I had been taught at least twenty-two different symbols. Frans was making life much simpler by explaining these four symbols and four mantras. This showed me that the additional symbols that I had learned had been created or taken from other cultures and added to the Western system of Reiki.

In chapter four, I mentioned Reiki symbols and mantras. They require some explanation.

In Japanese, the word for symbol is *shirushi*. In all of the Reiki systems that I have learned, there are four major symbols. The first is the *choku rei*, what is always called the master or power symbol. In Japan, a *choku rei* is called a *jumon*, or mantra. A *jumon* is a sound that invokes a very specific vibration. *Jumon* should be chanted or spoken correctly, as even a slight alteration will create a different vibration, in turn producing a different manifestation. Mantras must be chanted three times when used in conjunction with symbols. When a symbol is being drawn, the name of the symbol, the *jumon,* needs to be said or chanted at the same time.

In the West, the characteristic of *choku rei* is power; in japan it is focus. Confused? Well this is one reason that some masters prefer that their students stick to only one system of Reiki. I prefer to expand my knowledge so that I can give my students a choice of which system they would like to learn—Western or Eastern.

The second symbol and *jumon* is *sei heki*, which has the characteristic of mental or emotion in the West and harmony in Japan. The third symbol and *jumon* is *hon sha ze sho nen*. This is used for distant healing in the West and for connection in Japan. The fourth symbol and *jumon* is *dai ko myo,* which has the characteristic of embodiment of mastership in the West and empowerment in Japan.

My intention is not to confuse, and I have included a list of resources at the back of this book for those who wish to learn more about the Reiki system.

Now I would like to explain the three *hara* center colors. The word "hara" literally means "stomach, belly, or abdomen." This is where our energy is stored and from where it expands throughout the whole body. The *hara* is three finger-widths below the navel. Fran explained that there are, in fact, two other *hara* points in the body: the heart and the third eye. By linking all three, we as practitioners can create unity and balance.

On the Shinpiden, I discovered an inner truth for myself about the Reiki systems that launched me on a serious spiritual journey and lifted my energy and consciousness to a much higher level than I had ever achieved before.

Frans and Bronwen Steine first studied as Reiki masters in a Westernized form of Reiki in 1998. The list of masters leading to me is as follows:

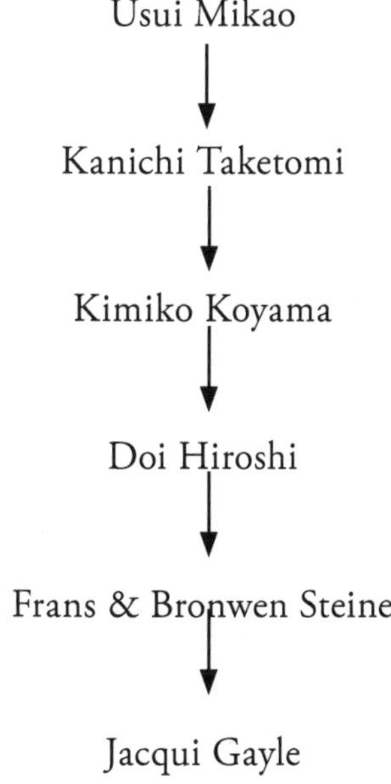

An Evening with Tadao Yamaguchi

Resonance is the name of the monthly magazine produced by the UK Reiki Federation. It is a regular bulletin of what is happening within the Reiki world, including events such as Reiki

Awareness Week, and it includes information on specialized courses and retreats.

In the summer of 2007, a particular item captured my attention and caused my whole body to come alive with positive energy. It read "an evening with Tadao Yamaguchi—come and hear a traditional Japanese Reiki master deliver a talk about his life and experiences with Usui Reiki Ryoho."

This was to take place in South Kensington, London, in October 2007. As you can probably imagine, I was on the phone straight away to book my place. Tadao Yamaguchi is the head of the Jikiden Reiki Institute in Kyoto, Japan, and he has more than forty years of experience. His family members were very involved with Reiki, and he first learned about Reiki from his mother, Chiyoko Yamaguchi, who was initiated by her uncle, Wasaburo Shugano, after he had received permission from Dr. Hayashi to do so.

I was so excited! All I could think about was that, at last, I would be meeting someone who had traditional Reiki experience and who could assist me in gaining greater insight into Japanese-style Reiki.

Soon I found myself in the presence of Master Yamaguchi. The master, through a charming interpreter, told the audience about his childhood and how his mother would gave him Reiki.

Master Yamaguchi continued to talk about his mother and the many people who came to his house to receive Reiki *ryoho* (Reiki treatment), and how he witnessed their gradual recovery from illness after several visits. After this talk, members of the audience were given the opportunity to ask questions regarding Reiki.

During the course of the evening, I had my photograph taken with Tadao Yamaguchi, and we talked via his interpreter, Rika, about Japan and the possibility of visiting there one day.

Before leaving the event, I gave Rika and her husband, Daniel, my contact details and thanked them both for a very informative evening with Tadao Yamaguchi.

In the days following that evening, I experienced a very deep peace and calm within myself, which brought me to an understanding of how far I had travelled since my days of turmoil and unhappiness and how the transition had been made smoother by the sheer presence of Reiki energy in my life. My intuition was sharper than it had ever been before, and my stress levels had become much more manageable with continuous self-treatment. To have something as powerful as Reiki energy in my life has been one of the greatest gifts life could offer.

About a month later, while checking my e-mail, I noticed a message from Rika advertising a Japanese tour in April 2008. I could not believe it. I felt so exhilarated. I turned to Philip and said, "I am going to Japan." Before you could say here I come, my check for my deposit was in the mail. On one level, this was simply another trip abroad, but on a personal level, I felt that it was a continuation of the spiritual path I had chosen.

Spiritual Keys

- *When you think a positive thought, mix that thought with positive emotions—happiness, joy, love, passion, and gratitude.*
- *Use the feeling of feeling good about yourself to help you in the creation of what you want from life.*
- *It is never too late to acquire specialized knowledge. We are all growth-seeking beings, and without learning, there is no growth.*
- *Once they leave school, a lot of people are unaware of the opportunities that further education can offer. There are numerous courses that could be suitable and lots of flexibility with part-time and evening options available. Visit your local library or look at the government-run programs to get ideas and further information about what is available.*
- *Books provide a powerful tool in the learning process, and many books are now available in electronic format.*

CHAPTER TEN

Japan

JIKIDEN REIKI

In April 2008, I arrived in Tokyo, Japan. The tour group was made up of eighteen people in addition to myself, from different parts of the world.

As a group, we took a bus to the Royal Park Hotel in Tokyo, and I had my first experience of Japanese politeness and organization. The driver and his team took our luggage and gave each of us a ticket that corresponded to a number on our individual pieces of luggage. This meant that we could collect our luggage quickly, without the usual fuss and mayhem.

After about an hour, we arrived at the hotel where we would be staying for the first two nights. At that time, I knew only two Japanese phrases: *konnichiwa*, which means hello, and *arigato*, meaning thank you. I met Annabel, a young English lady who I would be sharing a room with. Annabel met us at the hotel, as she had arrived earlier from Thailand.

Japan is such a clean country! For example, in our hotel, they had what was called toilet slippers. As you entered the bathroom, you would put the slippers on, and when you left, you took them off. I've been told it is impolite not to use these slippers, so I made sure I did. The people are humble, honest, and kind. They will go out of their way to help you.

I was so excited at the thought of the day ahead that I was up at five o'clock and I went for a quick swim, thinking I would be the only person at the pool, but, by five thirty, it was half filled with businessmen doing their daily routine of a few laps before going to work. When I arrived back at the room, Annabel had just woken up and was surprised that I had been for a swim so early. I explained to her that back in England, I went to the gym every work day to swim. We got ready and went down for breakfast, which was a combination of continental, English, and Japanese foods. At 9:30 a.m., we all congregated at reception and then we took the Tokyo Metro to Yoyogi Shibuya–Ku, where the Meiji Jingu is situated. Meiji Jingu is a shrine of national prayer for peace and prosperity. It was built as a result of combined efforts of the Japanese to commemorate the Emperor Meiji's virtues. This place is also known as a Shinto site; Shinto is a religion of Japan that emphasizes purification and respect.

In Japan, when entering a temple, it is considered polite to always enter from the right and leave from the left. Before you enter a temple or shrine, there will be a purification area known in Japanese as *chozubachi*. There will sometimes be a ladle and running water. You must take the ladle, fill it with the water, and wash first your left hand and then your right. You then use the remaining water to rinse out your mouth, spitting it out onto the gravel. You then need to let the gods know you are there to pray. If there is a temple bell, in the shape of a church bell, you pull the rope and ring it twice. If there is no bell, you can clap your hands twice instead. I believe that the first clap is to attract the attention of the sacred energies of heaven, and the second clap is to attract the sacred energies of earth. You must then bow, looking toward the earth, and say your prayer briefly. When you have finished, you must bow again.

I find it a beautiful ritual and one I will use on my return home in England. After spending some time at Meiji Jingu, we had lunch and got back on the Metro, heading for the Saihoji Temple. This was where we would find the memorial stone of Mikao Usui, which had many words written in Japanese. The words were written and the stone erected in 1972, a year after Usui's death. The stone talks of how Usui climbed Kurama and had twenty-one days of severe discipline and fasting. The stone mentions Usui's teachings and how popular he became through his Reiki system. After growing up, he visited Europe and America and studied in China.

We, as a group, were in awe of this memorial stone and wanted to have a photo taken, but we were told that this was not possible. I wondered to myself about that, because the memorial stone is pictured in many books and Reiki course notes around the world. I took a picture when no one was looking, and I'm glad I did, as it came in handy for the Reiki Council handbook!

The following morning, our suitcases were taken off our hands and forwarded to the Kokyu Hotel in Kyoto, where we would be staying. We took taxis to the train station, where we caught a bullet train to Kyoto. Visiting the restroom at the station, I noticed that the Western-style toilets had buttons that you could press to hear different types of sounds to cover up the sounds of other people using the toilet. To top that, the seats were heated! Before catching the train, we bought bento boxes filled with an authentic Japanese lunch, which we ate on the train.

As we waited for the train, I observed something heartwarming. A group of young people, in their early twenties, was sitting down next to me. Two elderly Japanese ladies came into the waiting room. The group of youngsters immediately stood up to offer their seats to the ladies, but their kind offer was politely refused. This went on for a few seconds, with the ladies continuing to refuse the offer. Then, the young people stepped outside, and the two ladies sat down in the now-vacant seats. The young people then returned to the waiting room and stood. It made me feel good just to observe it. It was amazing to see the level of respect people have for each other in Japan.

Our train arrived, and, once the passengers got off, another amazing thing happened. Cleaners appeared, dressed in pretty pink uniforms, and got to work cleaning every individual seat in the train, even wiping the windows. I had never seen anything like it. We were not allowed to enter the train until they had completed the cleansing process. I kept wondering what Japanese people must think when they come to England and use our tubes and trains or even walk down our streets in London.

Once we got to Kyoto and settled in the hotel, we all went to see Master Yamaguchi at the Jikiden Reiki Institute. On our arrival, the master greeted us and entertained us with green tea and sweets. We got a feel for the Institute and discussed what would be happening over the next few days, then we went back to our hotel.

We all had a relatively early night, except that Annabel and I started to bond as friends and we spent most of the night talking about the different styles of Reiki, our families, and our personal relationships. We eventually fell asleep, as we had to be back in the morning, ready to start learning, promptly at ten.

Day One

I was very excited about learning Jikiden Reiki. I consider it the crème de la crème, the ultimate system. To begin, we were taught the background to Jikiden Reiki seminars and we looked at some key Japanese words. We also covered the history of Reiki again.

Once Usui had attained enlightenment, he joyously ran down Mount Kurama. In doing so, he tripped over a rock that ripped off his toenail. According to the story, he happened to lay his hands on the nail, and suddenly the pain disappeared and it stopped bleeding. Amazed by this, Usui tried the laying-on of hands with his family, and he got great results.

Wanting to help others, he began research to find a method that would help him improve the mind, body, and spirit of others with Reiki (universal life force energy). This is known in Japan as *shin-shin kaizen*.

When Usui discovered his powerful healing technique, the word "Reiki" was already in use in Japan, so he called it Usui Reiki Ryoho, meaning method for improvement of body and mind, to make sure that people would understand that it was one discipline of the word "Reiki." I believe that the ability to heal spiritually has been in existence since the beginning of humankind. This is even evidenced in the Bible, where there are constant references to Jesus healing people. If Reiki is universal life force energy, then it must be part of the universe, which in turn is part of us as human beings.

During that first morning, we also learned that in April 1922, Usui moved to Aoyama Harajuku, which is quite near to the Meiji Shrine in Tokyo. There, he set up Usui Reiki Ryoho Gakkai. This was a study institute where he began teaching people by conducting seminars and giving Reiki treatments, which became very popular.

After lunch, we moved on to the objective of Jikiden Reiki and *gokai*, the five principles:

Western Principles
Just for today
Do not be angry
Do not be worried
Be grateful
Do your duties fully
Be kind to others
Japanese Principles
Kyo dake Wa
Ikaru na
Shin pai Suna
Kan Sha Shi te
Gyo—O hage me
Hito ni shin setsu ni

As part of the Japanese-style Reiki, students are taught *gassho*. This means placing both palms together when receiving attunements or meditating with Reiki energy. *Gassho* is not prayer and one does not need to believe in anything particular. *Gassho* is a Japanese gesture of respect. The *gassho* brings all opposites together, creating unity within the body by bringing the left and right hands together.

We moved on to chanting the five principles, and we received our first *reiju* for the day. Once this was completed, we sat in a circle, laying our hands on the person in front of us and concentrating on the sensation in our hands for ten minutes. We then took turns explaining what and how we felt; this is called Reiki *mawashi*.

Just before the session ended at 6 p.m., we experienced the giving and receiving of Reiki from one another. This provided me with feelings of deep relaxation and fulfillment.

With all Reiki teachers comes a Reiki lineage; here is my Jikiden Reiki lineage:

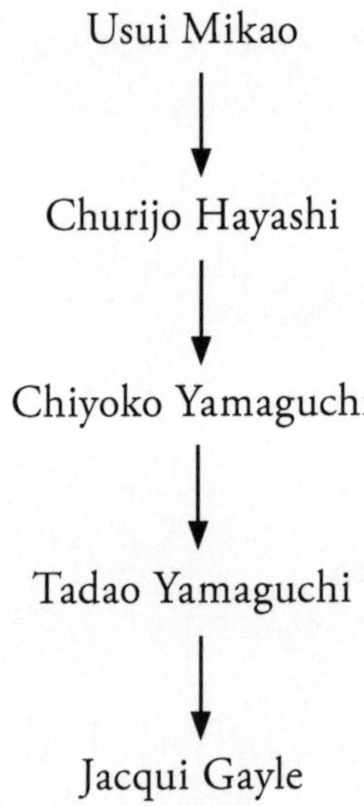

Day Two

I was looking forward to day two and feeling very positive that I would be gaining additional knowledge and learning different techniques, which I knew I could use when I returned to England.

We began with *reiju* and chanted the five principles, *gokai*, together. Afterward, we had our second *reiju* followed by Reiki *mawashi*.

It was at this point that the real lessons started for me. These taught us how to use Reiki to heal minor ailments. We were also taught the concept of *byosen*, whereby you learn how to feel the accumulation of toxins in the body. I found this quite fascinating, especially when we practiced on each other.

Reiki history shows that in the mid-1920s, Usui met Hayashi, who at the time was a retired naval officer. Hayashi spent most of his working life in the armed forces and, like some of us, walked a spiritual path. He was born September 15, 1880 in Tokyo, and in May 1925, he became a student of Mikao Usui. Hayashi practiced and experienced Reiki for some time under the guidance of Usui and other Mikao Usui members until he left to set up his own clinic and school. Dr. Chujiro Hayashi passed on the complete teaching of Reiki to two women, his wife and Madam Hawayo Takata, before his death in 1940.

Hawayo Takata was born in Hawaii on December 23, 1900, the daughter of Japanese parents. She was twenty-nine years old when her husband died, leaving her to bring up her two small daughters alone. She had started to lose weight and suffered poor health. In 1935, she went to Japan. I have heard many stories about Takata and how, while she was in Japan, doctors found that she had a tumor and needed surgery. Her own intuition told her that the operation would not be necessary, so she decided to speak with her doctor. She asked if there was any other way that she could be cured.

Apparently the doctor knew of Hayashi and his clinic. He told Takata about it. Takata decided to visit Hayashi, and she started to have regular treatments with him. Soon her health began to improve without the intervention of an operation.

Reiki had transformed her life and she asked Hayashi if he would teach her Reiki so she could teach it in Hawaii. At this time, Reiki had never been practiced outside Japan. After working with Hayashi for a year, Takata was initiated into second-degree Reiki. She returned to Hawaii to establish her own successful Reiki practice. Hayashi visited her there about two years later, ,and he confirmed her as a Reiki master or Shinpenden (a Japanese master level). She then became a well-known healer and was the first person to bring Reiki to the West.. It is said that, when she was seventy-five years old, she instructed others in the practice of Reiki and initiated twenty-two Reiki masters before her death in December 1980.

Back in the room, once again we chanted the five principles and received *reiju*. We then went straight into Reiki *mawashi* and then Reiki *okuri*, the method used to feel the Reiki energy flowing. We ended the day with the giving and the receiving of Reiki to and from each other. Most Western Reiki practitioners teach a basic twelve hand positions for treatments, regardless of whether there are any troubled areas to be healed. With Jikiden Reiki, students are encouraged to place their hands according to the sensations in the palms of their hands. This sensation can be felt where toxins are found in the body. In Jikiden Reiki this is called *Byosen*. Mr Yamaguchi explains that *Byo* means 'ill' or 'toxic' and *Sen* means 'lump' that disturbs the flow of energy in the body. So the word *Byosen* means a lump of toxins. If there is any sign of *Byosen* the practitioner will feel a tingling sensation in their palms and can heal accordingly.

Day Three

Everyone was on time and we started the third day with our daily chant of *gokai*, receiving *reiju*, and our practice of Reiki *mawashi*. We talked about *seiheki* treatment—Reiki used to help with psychological issues.

We then went on to practice giving and receiving *seiheki* treatment. I did not want the course to end, as I was learning so many new things that would help both my clients and myself!

Our next lesson was *enkaku* treatment. This is distant healing. We had an introduction to the subject and then we all practiced the technique. The experience was amazing. During the feedback discussion afterward, I discovered that I had been able to visualize what another person in the room had been thinking during the session.

Then we received our last session of *reiju* and we chanted *gokai* together and had Reiki *mawashi*.

The seminar was drawing to a close, and the time had arrived for the giving of certificates. I was the first to be called, and I was photographed sitting in front of Master Yamaguchi as he handed me two certificates, one in English and one in Japanese. At this moment, I felt so proud that I had made it to Japan to be taught by such a great man. I felt very blessed. Thank you Tadao Sensei.

Now our training was over, and it was time for some sightseeing. Saturday morning, bright and early, we set off to the Golden Pavilion, a temple properly called Rokuon-Ji Temple. What a beautiful sight, I have seen some amazing buildings on my travels but nothing as spectacular as this one. If you ever find yourself in Japan I strongly recommend that you make time to visit.

Our next stop was Sanjusangendo a temple famous for its 1001 statues of Senju Kannon, the goddess of mercy. We spent many hours there.

When evening arrived, we jump into a taxi to meet up with the rest of the group. Master Yamaguchi treated us to dinner with entertainment provided by Geisha ladies. A Geisha is a professional woman who entertains customers with various performing arts. To become a Geisha, a woman has to go through extensive training, where she acquires the skills, such as dance, singing, and playing three-stringed instruments. Their faces are painted, usually white as a base. The rest of the face is painted to give the girls a "china doll" look. We enjoyed great food, music, dancing, and we even played some games.

Eating in Japan was quite hard for me. I remember that, one evening, a group of us went out for a meal and I ordered egg-fried rice. What I actually got was a plate with raw egg and another plate with soggy rice. I dared not to order anything else for fear of what might turn up. I obviously did not know how to place an order correctly!

The following morning, we left the hotel to explore Mount Kurama. We arrived by minibus and were met by our guide, Mr. Kitano, a Jikiden practitioner. We gathered at the bottom of the mountain, and I tried to image what really happened back in March 1922, when Usui retreated here.

Kitano has studied various Reiki methods, including Western Reiki. He shared his thoughts with us, and his level of knowledge amazed me. I was completely overwhelmed by him. He talked about many subjects—some connected to Reiki and others that were not. It was at this point that I experienced my own enlightenment—a deep sense of what Reiki really means to me. I felt proud to be a practitioner and teacher of the energy healing art called Reiki, proud to be following in the footsteps of Mikao Usui.

Mount Kurama is 1870 feet above sea level. It is a very sacred place and has developed a rich tapestry of history and legend. Many people from all over the world make the pilgrimage to Mount Kurama to give thanks. It is 584 meters high and is one of the most enchanting places in the world. We saw wonderful tall trees and a site called Osugi Gongen, which is to the left, off of the main trail. This area has a small temple and a group of benches with lots of trees. It is said to be the place where Usui meditated for twenty-one days.

Some of the trees on Kurama are over one thousand years old, and some of the tree limbs have grown together, twisting and turning within each other. We also stopped to pray along the way. There are many shrines, springs, and waterfalls. We were given access to parts of temples that tourists do not usually see, and I am truly thankful to Kitano for this opportunity.

Kitano taught us how to set our fingers when we chanted and how to give ourselves a quick energy boost. Chanting places us in direct contact with our spiritual energy. For thousands of years, people have used mantras to elevate the mind and achieve states of spiritual consciousness.

Buddhism and Shinto are the two major religions in Japan. Mount Kurama has a combination of Buddhist and Shinto structures. A temple is a Buddhist structure, and a shrine is Shinto. The Shinto shrines are typically outdoors, with a *torii* near the site. A *torii* is a bird perch.

As for the temples you may visit, you are usually asked to take off your shoes. The Japanese are quite serious about their worship. Your shoes must be placed outside, on the concrete, facing away from the building. Visitors are asked not to take pictures inside the temple buildings.

Some hours later, we finally arrived at the top of Mount Kurama. We sat and had our lunch and took this opportunity to take photographs of and with each other. The energy on Mount Kurama is quite high, and one may become "spaced out" if not careful. I walked away from the group and stood staring at the trees, feeling the energy and giving thanks to the universe for allowing me to experience such wonder. I was amazed to discover that I had tears running down my face, tears of joy. I then made my way to the restroom. I experienced several different types of restroom facilities in Japan. The restrooms on Mount Kurama are squatter style, which literally means you have to squat. I found these to be the most hygienic.

Eventually, we walked back down the steep steps, still taking in the magnificent sights; finally before we knew it, we were back at the main street of Kibune, where we stopped for light refreshments and visited the shops. We then had a thirty-minute walk down to the train station, where we said good-bye to Kitano and thanked him for being our guide.

The train took us back to the bottom of Mount Katano and the waiting minibus, which conveyed us to a traditional Japanese *ryokan,* which is similar to a guesthouse. Onsen, the guesthouse (*onsen* means hot spring) has a spa with a natural thermal spring. It is a real Japanese-style accommodation. The entire place has been booked for our group for one night. It is said that the best time to visit is in the spring when the weather is at its finest. As soon as we arrived, we were each given a *yukata* (robe) to wear in and around the *ryokan*. The males of the group shared one big room, and the females shared four smaller rooms. The bedroom floors were covered with *tatami* (Japanese floor mats). No shoes or slippers are allowed on the *tatami*. There were no beds in the rooms, but while we had dinner, chambermaids brought out futon mats and thick, padded blankets. These were spread on the floor for us to sleep on. What a cultural experience! There was no central heating, however portable heaters are supplied in the winter months.

We immediately got into our *kimonos* and headed straight down to the *onsen*, which was a true delight. Swimming costumes are not allowed; only complete nudity. The men were on one side and the women on the other, but we could not see each other.

It was wonderful to step into a hot spring bath after such a long day at Mount Kurama. We all had a well-deserved late night of socializing, however I'm not sure that we all got what I would call a good night's sleep.

The following morning, a taxi took us to visit Katsura Imperial Villa. This is a cultural asset on the western side of Kyoto, and our visit there was a special treat that was arranged by a very kind Japanese lady who works for the Japanese Tourist Board and with whom we enjoyed a special contact. Mrs. Fukuhisa had sent us tickets that allowed us to visit this marvellous attraction. The villa has approximately seventeen acres that are beautifully landscaped, with a lake in the middle of the grounds and an intricate shoreline. It is impossible not to admire the natural beauty that can be witnessed. It is another sight that must not be missed when visiting Kyoto.

We then returned to Kyoto for lunch. I left the group and went to our hotel alone. I changed and walked down to Jodo Shinshu Hongwanji often referred to as Nishi Hongwanji, which is the mother temple and headquarters for more than twelve million Shin Buddhists affiliated with more than ten thousand temples and churches in Japan and throughout the world. I took my shoes off and went in.

There was chanting going on, so I sat with my hands together and began to chant, stopping only to meditate. I continued for a good hour and then I prayed and left.

I saw a bookshop just by the gate and I went in and browsed. I found two compact discs that I wanted to purchase, but I needed some advice and the assistant spoke no English. I remembered that one of the guards that I met outside the shop on my arrival spoke a little English, so I went to ask him if he could explain that I wanted to buy the discs but that I was not sure if they would work in the United Kingdom. The guard was also a little confused, so he used the shop assistant's telephone to contact an English-speaking friend of his to act as an interpreter for us. The phone was passed back and forth, and I discovered that one CD contains chanting and the other is wind music. I was truly amazed by the lengths the guard had gone to in order to help me, and I thanked him profusely for his help, which he understood.

I returned to my hotel feeling wonderful. Later that evening, we all met in reception for our last night out together as a group.

Early Tuesday morning, the minibus was waiting for us.

I honestly believe that Japan is a wonderful country with special people, though all countries have positive and negative sides. I would definitely love to return again someday.

The spiritual path that my life is now taking is on an upward spiral, the next step of which is to learn Eastern Reiki. I see myself as a being continually seeking to expand my knowledge. For me, there is no growth without new knowledge.

I have come a long way on my life's journey using Reiki energy to create changes in my life. I now feel a true sense of empowerment, contentment, and the knowledge that what I am doing with this beautiful energy is truthful for me. Continuous self-treatment with Reiki has given me so much self-belief and confidence. By drawing Ki within, I have cleansed and strengthened my inner self, allowing healing, not only for myself, but for others too.

By now you will have realized what Reiki healing means to me. Though some people believe that Reiki is in some way connected with the occult, this is not true and detracts from its integrity.

I would like to sum up what Reiki means with an easy acronym:

R-E-I-K-I-E-N-E-R-G-Y, with each letter outlining what I have managed to take on and utilize within my daily existence.

R= Review. If your life is all planned out and you know exactly what you are doing and where you're going then you may skip this one; for the rest, it's time to assess your life, with the intention of making change if necessary. Look at the areas in your life that are not working for you. Question yourself: what do you want from life? Remember that you only get one shot at it, so be honest with yourself, and when you have decided, stick with it and don't give up until you have achieved your goals. Use whatever resources you can—a prayer or affirmation will get the ball rolling.

E=Energize. Yes, that's right, get yourself some sort of healing, whether it's Reiki, crystal healing, yoga, swimming, dancing, bouncing on a trampoline, or making love—find something that will energize you. Something that will make you feel better within and about yourself.

I= Inspiration. Think about this one. Who are the people that inspire you? It could be your partner, your children, or a friend. Maybe a book that you have not got around to reading yet, or listening to a motivational speaker talk about a subject you are interested in is what will get you inspired. It might even be holiday snapshots of somewhere really beautiful that you visited in the past. Get them out stick them where you can see them. Just get inspired with positive action.

K=Kindness. Show plenty of this one. I know from personal experience that the more kindness you give out, the more you will receive. Be unconditional with your kindness. I can hear some of you saying it's a dog-eat-dog world and each man for himself, but, honestly, it doesn't have to be that way. It is possible to be kind to one another.

I=Individuality. That's right; it's okay to be unusual, different, or unique. Not everyone is the same, and just because someone is not the same as you or what you would expect them to be, that does not mean you should fear the unknown in that person. The saying goes "like attracts like," but maybe it's time we started to attract individuality into our lives to create a more colorful and rewarding existence.

E=Ego. There is no room for ego when it comes to Reiki, as it has no part to play and it does not serve us well.

N=Nature. Animals appear to love Reiki, and we can use it to deepen our relationships with them. Reiki is used to heal cats, dogs, horses, and even goldfish! If you hold your hands against an aquarium wall or fish bowl for fifteen to twenty minutes, the energy will transmit through to the water. Plants and trees can also be healed by Reiki energy.

E=Expectations. Positive expectations can enhance your well-being. Always expect good things to happen. Sometimes it is okay to lower your expectations, but never lower your standards. Be respectful to others, and expect the same in return.

R=Release. Let go of anything that is not serving you well in your life. That can be anything from people who are holding you back to over-indulgence in food, tobacco, alcohol, spending, gambling—anything that does not make you happy. If something or someone is making you unhappy, get rid of it.

G=Growth. Nothing gives me more pleasure than personal growth. Knowledge is powerful and empowering; learning new things in life gives us the will to learn more, and the more we learn from the whole universe, the more we grow mentally.

Y=Ying Yang. Where would we be without balance? In each male lies a feminine side, and in each female lies a masculine side. I chose to use this black and white symbol as part of my business logo to show that Reiki healing is here for both male and female clientele.

Spiritual Keys

- *If you are thinking of a country you would like to visit, don't just wish it; see it in your mind. Believe you can get there—don't allow yourself to think you cannot.*
- *If you think you can afford something, you never will be able to. Think positively; go and get some brochures, inquire about it, and research it. Perhaps you could download a picture of it from the Internet.*
- *See yourself lying on a beach or climbing up a mountain. Do whatever it takes to prepare you for this trip. Whatever it is that you desire, think it, believe it—and it will be yours. Remember that you are the master of your thoughts.*
- *Remember, world history was made on November 5, 2008 when Barack Obama was elected as president of the United States of America, showing the world that anything is possible if we just believe.*
- *To live a life filled with joy and enthusiasm, you will need lots of energy. Reiki will give you that energy.*
- *Finally I would like to leave you with one final quote: "Our greatest glory is not in never falling but in rising every time we fall."* Confucius (551-479 BC)

Resources

Balens
Specialist Insurance Brokers
2 Nimrod House
Sandy's Road
Malvern
Worcestershire
WR14 1JJ
(44+) 01684 893006
www.balens.co.uk

The Complementary Medical Association
Blackcleuch
Teviothead
Hawick
TD9 0PU
(44+) 0845 129 8434
www.cma.org.uk

Time2Heal
Bell Farm
Dunstable Rd
Studham
Bedfordshire
LU6 2QG
(44+) 01582 873334
www.time2heal.co.uk
www.Jacquigayle.com

The UK Reiki Federation
PO Box 71
Andover
Hampshire
SP11 9WQ
(44+) 01264 791441
www.reikifed.co.uk

The General Regulatory Council for Complementary Therapies.
Box 437,
Office 6 Slington House
Rankine Road
Basingstoke
Hampshire
RG24 8PH
(44+) 0870 3144031
HYPERLINK "http://www.grcct.org/"www.grcct.org

The Reiki Association
108 Augustus Road
London
SW19 6ER
07704270727

The Reiki Council
C/o 4 Westminster Court
81 Albermarle Road
Beckenham
Kent
BR3 5HP
www.reikicouncil.org.uk

Suggested Book List

Chopra, Deepak
The Soul of Leadership: Unlocking Your Potential for Greatness, London:
Rider, an Imprint of Ebury Publishing, 2010

Holland, Ron
Talk and Grow Rich: How to Create Wealth Without Capital, Chatham, Kent:
Thorsons, 1998

Jeffers, Susan
Feel the Fear and Do It Anyway, Vauxhall, London:
Vermilion an Imprint of Ebury Press Random House 2007

Miller, Jessica A.
Reiki's Birthplace, Sedona, California:
Infinite Light Healing Studio Centre Inc., 2006

Petter, Frank Arjava
The Original Reiki Handbook of Dr Mikao Usui, Twin Lakes, Wisconsin:
Lotus Press, 1998

Ray, Barbara
The Reiki Factor, St. Petersburg:
Radiance Associates, 1983

Shine, Betty
Mind Magic, Ealing, London:
Corgi Books, Transworld Publishers, 1991

Steine, Bronwen & Frans
The Reiki Source Book, Oakland, California:
O Books, 2004

Steine, Bronwen & Frans
The Japanese Art of Reiki, Ropley, Hants:
O Books, 2005

Steine, Bronwen & Frans
Your Reiki Treatment, Ropley, Hants:
O Books, 2007

Turner, Barry
The Writers' Handbook, New York:
Macmillan, 2010

Wenham-Jones, Jane
Wannabe a Writer, Mid-Glamorgan:
Accent Press, 2007

Whitelaw, Stella
How to Write and Sell a Book Proposal, Woodston, Peterborough:
Writers' Bookshop - an Imprint of Forward Press Ltd, 2000

Yamaguchi, Tadao
Light on the Origins of Reiki, Twin Lakes, Wisconsin:
Lotus Press, 2007

Printed in Great Britain
by Amazon.co.uk, Ltd.,
Marston Gate.